MW00326070

"Sandra's story of a mother's jo... daughter is heartwarming and ... a parent in a similar situation. I highly recommend this to anyone who wonders what it's like to be a loved one who watches and is learning to support the child they brought into the world become the human being they were meant to be. A must read for all."

> —**Renee Settle**, National Chapter Director
> Non-fiction Authors Association/
> Ghostwriter/Speaker/Publishing Consultant

"...(my) first impressions concern the ease and descriptive ability of Sandra's prose... Few aspiring authors are able to write large works so syntactically uncluttered that reading feels akin to drinking. That is, it's natural, easy, even automatic... (and) inviting... (she's) got both the writing chops *and* an emotionally-charged story... The story is difficult but authentic and it is brave to tell."

> —**Craig Holder**, author of *Matala*,
> *The Narcissist's Daughter* and *The Jazz Bird*

"*She Had Been a Tomboy* is one mother's loving, emotionally-charged story of finding out that her troubled child is transgender. Bowman's narrative is impassioned and determined. She exhibits strong support for her child's gender identity and her struggles; her ache of watching Grace suffer is palpable. The author's consistent message of loving and accepting your child unconditionally is uplifting."

> —**BlueInk**

"Sandra Bowman delivers this story with poise and conviction, and the reader feels throughout that [they] are receiving the unfiltered truth... Sandra's enthusiastic love and her dedication to her daughter's happiness shines in this memoir"

> —**Independent Book Review**

SHE HAD BEEN A TOMBOY

Raising A Transgender Child,
A Mother's Journey

SANDRA BOWMAN

Published in the United States by Sandra Bowman together with PFG-LLC,
Seattle, WA, in 2022

This is a work of nonfiction. Events are to the best of the author's recollection. The names
have been changed to protect the privacy of individuals.

Library of Congress Cataloging-in-Publication Data

Name: Bowman, Sandra, author
Title: She had been a tomboy raising a transgender child, A mother's journey/ Sandra Bowman
Description: First edition. Seattle, Washington. Sandra Bowman with PFG-LLC, 2022
Identifier: LCCN 2022905216
Subject: Parenting, LGBTQ+ issues, family
Classification: Print

ISBN: 978-0-578-34951-0 (paperback)

Cover design copyright © 2022 by Richard Ljoenes Design LLC
Interior design by KUHN Design Group | kuhndesigngroup.com
Edited by Kristen Hamilton. Kristen Corrects, LLC

Printed in the United States of America

Sandra Bowman

Dedicated to all who wonder…

author's note

I have a daughter. She is beautiful. She is remarkable. She stands six feet, five inches tall. This, undoubtedly, is remarkable in itself. But then added to this remarkable is the fact that s(he) came into the world tiny, uniquely tiny. She grew from very small to very tall. Of course this was a natural progression, one over which she held no sway.

Reluctantly, believe adversely, I have referred to my daughter as s(he). I did so, however, because there was a time when even I believed my daughter was my son. My eyes told me this. Her physicality told me this. And this is the reason I refer to her as "him" when I write about her childhood years, those years before I came to understand otherwise. But it was later, twenty-four years into the future, when I learned this had never been the case, her being male. Despite what her body once presented to me, to herself, to the entire world, for two and a half decades, her brain has always known the truth.

Still, as concerns the greater population, there remains two disparate beliefs regarding this matter of when my *son* "became" my daughter. On one side are those who (not necessarily with malice) believe my daughter was once my son, or rather, that my daughter has not always been female. More often than not, these same individuals hold that it was at some particular point in time when she decided to change genders.

On the other side stands the truth.

And this truth? This is the *fact* that my daughter is truly my daughter. The *fact* that my daughter, she has *always been* my daughter. And her gender as female has been true from conception, all during utero, at birth, and every stage going forward. There has never been a gender for her otherwise and, just as her "small to tall," there has never been a choice involved whatsoever.

But as for her childhood years, those years of unknowing, they were filled with obstacles that threatened to tear the two of us apart. These were obstacles that threatened to tear our entire family apart. I now know, with all adult certainty, that when one is broken all are broken.

I know what it means to face defeat.

Ours is a story of confusion, of misunderstanding, of not knowing how to help, how to "fix." It is a story of not seeing what it is that needs fixing. It is about years of trial and of error. Of disappointment. And failure.

Clearly my mothering has not been a smooth journey; neither does it have a touch of the allure simply for its otherness. It is, rather, one of struggle and continuous uncertainty, fear and heartache.

Although in grand opposition, ours is also a story of growth and redemption. We, as a family, are becoming whole again. We are becoming a family again, albeit in a way different than we began.

I'm not here to shame; I'm not here to blame. I merely want

to speak the truth, in the case you don't yet know this. Or, if you don't mind hearing again what you have known all along.

Respectfully,
Sandra Bowman

introduction

I think back to a time beforehand, my mid-twenties. Naturally I consider those years since those were the exact years I came to figure every bit of it out. They were, in fact, the years I came to *plan* every bit of it out...all this mothering confusion. My twenties, that was a time I knew all. A time I was able to see the future and recognize the power over it I held. Those were years when the path forward stood clear, intact, and effortlessly mine.

Inevitably then I think back to my childhood. My mind drifts there too.

Another beforehand time.

I consider the events that led to establishing my mothering plans...

I am three.

I see steaming pot roast, I *smell* steaming pot roast. Browned potatoes. I eye the canned string beans (from these I look away). I am hungry. Very. Hungry. I have always been skinny. And I am active. Busy, and forever moving about. I want a *feast*.

The kitchen is warm with cooking. The windows are opaque

due to steam and the contrasting outdoor cold. The room is relaxed, tranquil. Expectant.

We're around the table, my parents, my three siblings and me. My brother Danny, older by three and a half years, quietly, subtly *just about* empties the milk. This is what he does before discreetly pushing the carton my way. This is what he does because he knows it will be me who will greedily take the last few drops, which means, of course, I will be required to get up and bring back a fresh carton. This he does because this will be funny and, therefore, he will benefit from a laugh as the joke on me unfolds. In any case, even at three, I have lived this scenario over and again, these various incidents of "funny." And at these times I easily witness all his joy. Therefore this is simply one more amusement he designs to incite yet another of my anticipated, say never-to-disappoint, breakdowns. And this "breaking down" part of the ritual…well, this is the bit that is *really funny*.

And so presently, as continuously, I remain devoted to the role he has given me in his comedy. And my endless role devotion? It seems this is funny as well.

And I ignite. This, of course, due to the taunting, the laughing, the production itself. But then, seeing as my mother and older sister also have their fixed roles in the performance, they keep with my brother's script as well.

And so this is the moment my mother attempts to neutralize clamorous me.

And with eternal solidarity, this is when my sister begins to glare menacingly at me. Trouble-making me.

And they are exasperated with me.

Again and forever it is me my mother is exasperated with.

I enter puberty. I feel hollow, uncertain. I *need*. I need a reassurance of love. I need this from my mother. I need her to soothe me. My emotions, my fear of her separateness, these extend everywhere. Do I know my body is shifting? Fluctuating? No. Yes. No. Despite the recent integration of sex education in the classroom I don't think I'm altogether aware of my experience. But yes, I *feel* different. I feel alone. I feel fear. I feel confusion.

My mother stands before the stove. She is stirring sauce for spaghetti. The look on my face is pained as I approach her. My body says this too. She looks over when she hears me nearing and this is the moment I ask for a hug. My sloping posture alone begs this of her. But my emotions, the *depth* of my emotions, these overwhelm her. Frighten her.

Best to pretend all is fine.

She turns to me next. Her upper arms remain close by her sides but then lift upward at the elbows. And her wrists, they turn outward and level, horizontal to the floor, all this to show incredulity. Her incredulity.

"What's wrong?" She shrugs her shoulders next, this adding emphasis to the disbelief she feigns, this to defend her need of detachment. Her voice itself is judgement rendering me silent, frozen. She turns away next, looks down at the stove, tending wholeheartedly to her stirring.

I remain beside her. Tears begin.

Still my mother, she wills her thoughts elsewhere and, in this manner, she lets known every bit of the shame I now feel. Shame over my emotions, *over the strength of my emotions*, over this continuous and exhausting need of her. She carries on, her sole focus with her sauce, her stirring; the protection of herself.

She hasn't time for a hug.

I walk away.

There is nowhere safe.

My mother sits in the center of our living room among her four children. She cradles the baby, this is my brother Steven who is six months now. The rest of us are running or tottering about. I am twenty months. My sister Megan has recently turned three. Danny, he is five. Barely.

As for my mother herself?

By this time, she is all of twenty-four.

The most significant event in my life? *The* defining incident that shaped my childhood? My life? Well, in fact, this is an event that never happened to me, but rather, to my mother. Although, more accurately, it was the aftermath of this event that came to truly injure her, and later injure me. The aftermath. *This* is what defined *my mother's* childhood, *her* life. And this is what continues to conquer the two of us to this very day.

I am nine; this is going to be my ninth Christmas and I am afraid. I am afraid of the coming of Christmas because on Christmas Day it is certain my mother is going to die.

And it was Christmas then too, or rather, Christmas Eve, early evening, this the time of the event. My mother's mother is with a group of coworkers. One of these companions is driving as the five make their way from that season's holiday office party. They cross a bridge and this is when the car hits ice and begins its spin. Seatbelts? No. This was the '40s.

They strike a guardrail, hard.

The passengers are jolted, *thrown*, by the force. Nevertheless, it is my grandmother alone who is taken to the hospital for observation, her impact having been the greatest. During that evening's visit my grandfather, my mother, and her older brother alike are given a pass. My grandmother will be home the next morning for Christmas celebration.

She dies during the night due to internal bleeding.

My mother is nine.

I have seen pictures of my grandmother in her youth, and then at the age she died. Without a detail amiss I am her identical twin. My mother will forever see her mother when looking at me.

This too is between us.

As for the subsequent tragedy? My grandfather will send my mother away; she will live elsewhere. Falling to pieces will not be tolerated. Any additional pain for him would be unbearable. At nine she doesn't understand this. What she does understand is that tears, adverse emotion in general, these are treacherous. Any display of sorrow, of needing him, these will be the reason she will lose both her parents. A lesson lastingly imprinted.

My mother then guards her tears, her pain, close and in private. With a childhood fear equal to life and death she does this. But her father, he creates the distance he needs: from her, from any possible trace of her suffering, from any possible display of grief or tears. He stays away. His work days become long and longer still. And, it is in this way, he abandons her even so.

She is alone.

There is nowhere safe.

As concerned me later? My grandmother's twin? The trouble-maker among us? A daughter desperate to be folded into the intimacy my mother and sister shared exclusively? Without me... my mother will be unable to tamper her fear, her panic, over *my* emotions. She will be incapable of offering comfort. She will be unable to do other than to distance herself. And, it is in this way, she abandons me just the same.

Then, later still, while in my twenties? Those promising years when I established my mothering plans...and every pledge I made then, all set in place in order to assure I would be a different sort of mother than that of which my own was capable?

Well the future, it seems, has plans of its own.

While promises...even those made with yourself? They too find a way of falling to pieces...

Robert

The evening I meet Robert is the end of a long day. There are ten of us. Having just moved a friend into her new place, we are exhausted. This after hours of driving and hauling. This is furniture, overstuffed boxes, stacks of clothes. All driven over from her former place. Our legs are tired from the too many stairs we have climbed, descended and then climbed again.

And we are famished.

Robert holds up a long wooden pole as he enters. Attached to this pole is *string*? *fishing line*? which is tied on either end and hangs downward in an arc. Dangling vertically from this line are two dozen or so trout. Some small. Some rather large. It is a semi-circle, a bow of sorts of fresh fish. A flash of pattern and shape. Of muted, then vibrant color. A moving, fleeting masterpiece. Of fish. Wild and that day fresh.

And we are famished!

As if he is able to *see* our hunger, Robert begins preparation for the feast we will all share. Wine is opened. Potatoes have been discovered. Someone runs out in search of the makings for salad.

He is at the stove, Robert, which is wide open across a half wall. Three of us stand on the opposite side facing him, watching him cook. He raises his head then and he grins. (*He's pretty cute.*)

The three of us grin back. Stupidly.

At the table he sits across and two spaces down from where I am seated. He glances over from time to time in my direction. He smiles again, he thinks I'm funny. He laughs.

(*Okay yes, he is cute.*)

It is two days later when we ski. Not all ten of us, or now eleven, but this is only Robert and I who head to the pass. We have dinner out. We cook. We see movies, plays. We hang out, content in doing nothing side by side.

He buys a house.

A year later we marry.

He isn't sure he wants children. This conversation occurs as we sit overlooking the water talking about our future together. The evening is warm, all wide-open sky and constellations. The water is thirty feet or so below the grassy incline where we talk. High tide. We have just come from one of our many dinners out.

I tell him I'm certain I want children. Yes, I absolutely *know* I do. (*I will do it differently than my mother, better. I will do it right!*)

I have a plan…

He comes around to the idea of children. In truth, not too much time passes before he does this.

Two years later Grant is born.

When Grant is twenty months I am pregnant with Parker.

And, setting aside the three cats and two dogs we will adopt along the way, this is our family.

And we know we are lucky to have this family.

We are extraordinarily lucky.

one

The Early Years

I stand with my son before a human-sized device situated within the mathematics division of the Museum of Science. He is five.

Throughout mathematical and scientific communities everywhere this device models what is known as normal distribution. This particular device is filled with what look to be ping-pong balls, one hundred in all. When a button is pushed, the balls that are then released fall in a distinct and predictable pattern. This is the virtually never-varying pattern of normal distribution. There is a hole, just one, situated above the many slots of the machine. Underneath this hole and above the slots are pegs spread in such a way so as to make a triangle shape where the point reaches upward. The triangle hovers above the openings and its expanse is the exact width of the extent of the slots below.

There are two openings beneath this hole that embrace the center. Reaching outward from this center, the walls gradually and evenly shorten so that when looked upon give off a sloping pattern that resembles the shape of a bell.

As each ball in turn descends within this device, its initial tap will be against the uppermost peg of the triangle. It is in this moment when it has a fifty-fifty chance of falling to the right of the apparatus or to the left. As follows the natural rules of this pattern, the majority of these balls find themselves situated within one of the two center holes. The rest then distribute themselves in a precise way so that the end result consistently gives the onlooker the bell. The farthest-reaching balls on either end are singular. They are the two unique, isolated balls out of every one hundred.

Grant is four. I am driving. He sits in his car seat behind and his mind is set on matters that do not resemble those of other children his own age. When he speaks he informs me that twelve times twelve equals one hundred forty-four. Although I am becoming accustomed to the depth of knowledge my son seems to pull out of nowhere, or everywhere, or God knows where, I am still undeniably astonished. When he speaks again he describes the system in which negative and positive numbers proceed as they pass back and forth along the numbered spectrum. He explains that the pattern changes depending on whether one uses addition and subtraction or multiplication and division.

"When added," he says, "two positive numbers will always move further into the positive." He affirms that the combination of a negative and a positive number, whether added or subtracted, will rest closer to the highest number given. "But Mommy," he asks, "did you know that when two negative numbers are multiplied they will magically turn positive?"

And to be honest, I'd forgotten I'd ever learned that.

Five again.

Inside the Museum of Science, we move toward a hall where a presentation on our solar system will soon begin. As we assemble I note that Grant is the youngest in the room. The majority of the audience is comprised of a large group of students, middle school-aged, out of class on a field trip. Grant, however, does not notice the others around him because it has never occurred to him to do so. As he sits forward in his chair it seems he will slide off as he squirms in anticipation of the lecture. He does, in fact, slide off, not one slip, but three. And between slips he bounces on the cushioned seat beneath him as eagerly he conveys to me his knowledge of the planets.

"They forever rotate and behave as if tethered to their spots, Mommy," he continues, "but also they seem to float at will in a limitless space. But they can't leave, Mommy, and that's because of the gravitational pull of the sun."

The lecturer points to every planet in succession and the audience is asked to shout out the name of each world she rests on. Foreseeably the older children amuse themselves with this, as it contradicts the strict rule of the classroom. Freely they mock convention; they joke and they laugh. They are unaware they are being manipulated into engaging in the process of learning. In contrast, there is no joking around with my very young son. He takes his responsibility earnestly as he attempts to holler above the combined voices of the crowd. As the lecture progresses he continues to speak, ever loudly in order to answer every question available. His answers are correct, insightful and delivered with excruciating sincerity.

But there is one, as I now know there will always be one,

among the older children who asks my son from across the hall if his head is up "Uranus?" The cruel hilarity that follows is just a sliver, a mere crumb placed before me in order to lead me toward the truth.

This then is the truth of the tragic and ultimately terrifying abuse my son will receive as he moves throughout his life.

Because my child is the farthest-reaching ball.

Birth Days

I lie on my back. My head rests downward and my feet are raised so as to be elevated high above the rest of me, as high above my head as is sound. I've been in this position for exactly one week.

As do all long-term "residents" of this hospital, I have a primary nurse assigned to my case. I have been stationed here now for two and a half months. My nurse is fair, blotchy, with freckled skin and saggy arms. She is thick around the middle and sweaty with menopause. She is sturdy and determined and comfortingly bossy. When checking my temperature for the third time before lunch she touches my brow and stokes me near the hairline.

She turns to leave the room next, and I notice her leaving is not without some haste. An orderly arrives with a gurney. Having preceded him back into the room by an instant my menopausal nurse boss hovers about reassuringly. I am asked to heave-ho as I am raised and then lowered onto my new device. I am headed for delivery.

The room is huge, cold and serious. As my lower body starts to numb from the injection I take note of the literally dozens of people surrounding my bed busy attending to God knows what. They make up a huge, cold, serious crowd swarming within a huge, cold, stainless steel room. This *is* serious. And those are exactly my doctor's words as he instructs me to push. This one attempt is discouragingly fruitless and so next, coming very close to my ear, my doctor speaks in a quiet, no- messing-around voice when he says, "*Damn it Sandra…push!*"

It is minutes after this second command when my son is born. He is early by three months and his birth weight is exactly two pounds, nine and a half ounces. He is fighting for his life. He has been on this Earth for a nanosecond and already he is fighting to survive his tiny, isolated world. His private world of agony.

The oxygen that is necessary for his survival is administered at once, even before he is cut from my body. But I don't witness this. I'm not allowed a glimpse. He has left the room, been taken from me, removed from my womb and I don't put my eyes on him for two hours. I don't put my hands on him for two days. The pain would be excruciating but for my surge of "*happy*," say "*euphoric*" hormones. And thankfully euphoria will remain within me and it will care for me for the entirety of the next two weeks.

Within the hour I am back in my room. I lie on my bed here, in this room. A room that has been mine for over two months now. This is where I *am*, and this is where I will *remain* until I am granted permission to see my son. But too, and in idyllic contrast, the sun enters. It greets me here, offers a welcome glow, an added warmth. It, in fact, stirs in me something akin to laughter. This is September, a September coming off a summer that had been exceptionally dry, unusually hot. And despite the drought, the relentless heat that had baked this room most of July into August, the sun for me is yet another something to cheer about.

I am everything that is unrestrained joy.

I have no clear idea I will not hold my son that day, that he won't be swaddled, brought to my room and placed into my ready arms. He won't be wrapped in my embrace, no. Not like the blissful scenes in movies, not like the perfection of the movies. This is not like that.

I want to spin. Handspring! My laughter is irrepressible.

Two hours pass before I am wheeled into the newborn ICU. The lighting here is dim. As I've just come from the outside corridor, my eyes need time to adjust. Even so I notice straight away the tiny button-sized lights that are attached above each infant's station. Some are yellow, others blue. A number are red. They flash and they beep at irregular intervals. This is the place I see my son. Underneath these lights. This is where he is and this is where he will stay.

I will not swaddle him. Not today.

My smile grows enormous.

It is an instant before I see he looks like his father, despite his tiny size, although his head that is narrow due to its preemie softness. It is regardless of all that I am able to determine this. He lies inside a glass box. Out of reach. No permission to touch. Just gaze, which I'm allowed to do for one hour before I'm directed to leave the room. The ICU, the scene of it, all the commotion surrounding me, my son with his many, many wires and needles, tubes and alarms, the rows upon rows of infants who lie in boxes, the nurses who rush about…all this may overwhelm. I don't know this yet. Robert pushes the wheel-chair forward.

My speech is fast, my talking is non-stop.

I cannot remember Robert's reaction. To the birth. Our son's miniature frame, the dashing him off. The multitudes of helpers at his side as he is taken from me. The oxygen they held, the many monitors and instruments they carried, those that would keep his heart in check, his temperature stable. My memory, it refuses to offer up one thing as concerns Robert then, what he thought. How he felt.

Because I am euphoric.

I am pacing in my room now, this after visitation hour. Again this room which is all too familiar. My room with its ceiling stain. A two-inch rust-colored blemish I have now stared at for weeks on end. Here is where I pass the time together with the chip in the door frame that grumbles to me, demanding my attention as well. But regardless of all, it is happily that a friend is waiting. My family hasn't arrived yet but never mind, because my exuberance has taken over the whole of me and causes my mind to soar. My language cannot keep up with my thoughts. I stride now. I want to jump. I am a tower rising above all. Robert? Rene? Neither mirrors what I am feeling. Still, despite their reserve, everything that can be right is right. Every bit of their quiet is inconsequential. I continue to ascend.

Hormones.

These are a powerful presence.

He spends two months in the ICU inside his box of glass.

There is an arm-sized opening on one side of his isolette. This hole is surrounded by a hospital shade of icy-green enclosed rubber through which, in two days' time, I am able to reach inside. This in order to touch him, this in order to gently place my hand on his tiny back. And I leave my hand just there for hours upon hours. This is the replacement for his mother's swaddle. With the exception of the occasional hurried stroke provided him by a passing nurse, this is his sole human contact for two weeks. The two weeks that pass before I am able to hold him. The two weeks that pass before euphoria no longer protects me.

He is wrapped in a small blanket for his first outside excursion. The necessary cover wraps around him several times so when he's placed into my arms it is in distinct mummy-style. His head is protected with a stocking cap to prevent escaping body heat. Wires and tubes connect him to his isolette even now. Wires reach out from inside his blanket near his head, his neck, and stretch back. A nurse stands beside me, beside Grant. She holds a flexible tube, one she has uncoiled to reach out. She keeps this near Grant's nose and mouth all the while I embrace him. This contains the oxygen he needs. I kiss him and I stroke his face, I rock him and I sing to him. But this holding, this lasts a total of fifteen minutes before he is again taken from me and placed back into his box of glass. This holding is not allowed every day. I must wait two more days before I am able to hold him again.

Now is the time I can hardly speak, I can hardly breathe. By now, I can barely stand upright.

He has no hair, he has no cartilage in his ears which lie flat and Spock-like in appearance. His tiny cries are scarcely audible. The blood pressure band used to wrap around his upper arm barely surrounds my tiniest finger. He forgets to breathe and his heart forgets to beat. Alarms sound and knowing nurses stride toward his isolette to tickle his foot. Only then does he remember his lungs and his heart. His digestion is working full tilt! His dime-sized poops are proof. But I watch anxiously as his nervous system develops. Calmly, it is explained, that his troubling and his constant and his irregularly-timed body spasms are just that.

His isolette is warm, exceptionally so. His thin skin demands this, skin that is nearly translucent. He wears no clothes save a miniature diaper, or rather, something similar to a hospital mask, one otherwise purposed to cover a doctor's mouth and nose, only much smaller. Any additional covering would restrict access to his heart, his lungs, his veins.

He lies on his front. His legs spread wide but are turned inward at the knee so that his feet nearly touch, so that from the waist down his shape resembles that of a frog or the first stage of a breaststroke. Sensors have been positioned on his back and on his head in order that alarms will sound when he has the need to be tended, the call to be tickled. His blood requires checking regularly. Pins are placed that pierce his veins for this purpose. A staff member adjusts to unused veins periodically to give relief, to avoid infection. There are days when needles are protruding from his forehead. He looks in constant pain. I whisper to him, I tell him I love him. I place my hand on his fragile back. I lower my head and I close my eyes.

I have an abundance of milk to provide him and I must pump my milk as much to relieve my discomfort as to afford him my nourishment and the antibodies that come with it. The milk is stored in one-ounce bottles, dated, sealed then placed in the cold. I throw some away when there is no more room inside the added freezer we have bought solely for this purpose. Each shelf holds hundreds of these tiny red-capped bottles and our freezer is brimming full. I will carry these tiny bottles containing my milk to the hospital in a small ice chest when needed.

But for now I am directed to a room next to the ICU where I will pump my milk. This way I provide the staff with it immediately. For now a gavage tube is used to guide the milk inside my child. When it's time for feeding, the tube jutting from his mouth is connected to another tube which is connected to a pump. Gently then the milk is pushed down the tube which runs through his esophagus and to his stomach. The lower half of the tube remains within him constantly. For this reason his mouth is perpetually open and continuously dry. This method of feeding persists for over a month. Afterward, for the final three weeks of his stay, he learns to suck on his own. His mouth is too small to latch on to me but he is able to suck from the very small bottles topped with the very small nipples from our freezer. "His suck is strong," I am told. "He has the instinct for survival."

There is a sterile gown and cap I take from a cupboard which I adorn before entering the ICU. There are covers for my shoes. I must scrub for twenty minutes, I must *scour* for twenty minutes, and it is required that this scouring includes my arms up to my elbows. The liquid soap is honey-colored. The smell is stringent and assaults my nose. It is everything that is caustic and abrasive. I must clip my nails often; it is essential they remain as short as possible so as to avoid spreading germs. Still, each day I unwrap a sterile brush that I use to clean under my non-nails. I am required to scrub one at a time, staying with each at minimum thirty seconds. At home I apply lotion, a lot of lotion, although in truth this makes little difference in battling against my damaged hands, my wounded lower arms. Often I will scrub twice a day. For two months my skin, this on my hands, my arms, is raw.

There are intervals when I leave the ICU. This for brief periods. I lie down then on a low bed in an undersized room situated across the corridor from the newborn ICU. This room is available for parents in order to rest up, nap. In order to collect themselves. Afterward again I sit beside him, my tiny son. Just sit with his stillness, he inside his box. I return my hand to his back and once more keep it there for hours, up until the time a nurse gently suggests, "Go, get something to eat, rest." I cry every day as I abandon him. My heart aches for him, aches to hold him.

A large wall of glass opens onto the corridor outside the newborn ICU. Newly formed birthing classes are led through this corridor in order to glance inside, in order to familiarize themselves with this room. Just in case. They glimpse a sea of monitors, an endless sea of blinking, buzzing monitors. They shade their eyes and press against the glass in order to view beyond and through the muted lighting put in place so as to protect the eyes of the fragile infants inside. They see rows of tiny, tiny people inside glass boxes.

"The chances are small," they are assured.

On the other side of the glass wall, the mothers of babies who cannot survive on their own turn away. There is difficulty in viewing these women. Those mothers-to-be who know how to care properly for their unborn children, just as all mothers should. Those naturally competent women who grant their infants appropriate time to prepare for the outside world. As for those of us on the inside? The classes timed perfectly for our tours would have begun the previous, or the current, or the following week. And this would have been if only we had done things right.

He develops anemia. This has come about because my iron was not naturally passed to him during our "*would have been*" third trimester together, the final three months when my body would quite rightfully have nourished and strengthened his. Now after three weeks on the outside, his body cannot produce red blood cells on its own. "Anemia," the staff makes clear, "is something most preemies come to know."

A full blood transfusion is what he needs at present and we must sign to consent. Despite matching blood types, that of father and of son, this is a case where his father's blood cannot be administered. We talk to people higher and higher up the policy chain. But the answer is always the same. "Policy. Newborn Intensive Care Unit Policy," period. So as the transfusion comes to completion the blood that now flows throughout the entirety of our young son's body, every last drop, is that of a stranger's. For the remainder of his life he will share a blood type with his father, but also, until always, he will share genuine blood with someone we will never encounter again. We are thankful for the blood. We hope and still we fear. We worry further over whether the unknown donor's blood is clean.

It's a Thursday. I begin to scrub. A doctor comes out from inside the ICU and informs me that today I cannot enter. All blinds are drawn along the wide stretch of viewing windows.

So it is a long day and a wakeful night before I learn of the tiny babies, each one stationed on either side of my child's isolette, that had passed away the morning before. I had sat, and I had worried alongside these mothers for nearly two months. We had held hands and we had cried into each other's arms. Now they are gone. Without my condolences, dispossessed of a simple, fleeting embrace, they are gone. I cry and I cry. I nearly collapse with the weight of the pain and the exhaustion and the loss.

But my child is strong. His lungs, heart, and faithful digestive tract are ready to stand alone. He is not quite four pounds. As for me? Ready is the last thing I am. This for the simple reason that it had been only one day prior when a nurse had rushed to tickle his foot as he forgot to breathe. I am given no notice about his discharge until the very moment I arrive in the morning but, based on doctor's orders, it will happen now. A nurse, not my red-haired, freckled, menopausal nurse, but a young, hurried, silent nurse leads me to a room, my baby in my arms. My two-month, not yet four-pound fragile infant swaddled six times inside his tiny blanket, stocking cap protecting his head, is placed into my arms and we are led away from the safety of the ICU.

That evening he is placed inside a crib stationed next to my new hospital bed where we will spend one night, a nurse looking in only once. In comparison to that giant crib he is a mere speck, a tiny, tiny bundle swimming in a sea of padding. Then me listening to his quiet breathing. Placing my ear close to his face to double, triple, even quadruple check he is still alive, to make certain he will miraculously come home with me the following morning. Despite my exhaustion, sleep is not to be. In fact, sleep is not to be for a good time going forward.

Once home he needs sustenance every ninety minutes. Inside a pan of water placed on the stove, I warm one of the small red-capped bottles I now store in the refrigerator. It takes him forty-five minutes to finish one ounce of milk before falling back to sleep. I lie down and rest the remaining forty-five minutes, the time I have before he cries out in hunger again, and this becomes our routine each day and each night, for the next three months.

But ever steadily, as his weight increases, his feedings begin to spread out. At five pounds his hat can be removed and he is allowed some freedom from his blanket. I search for clothes, I rifle the "preemie" racks but the clothes look enormous. Graciously then my cousin makes doll clothes, "miniature people" clothes that without a breath of struggle one and a half of him could fit inside.

At eighteen months our pediatrician tells me he has "caught up" with most children his own age. Children who had been born the same month but had come into the world bearing weights depicting that of average newborns; "full-termers" who had weighed seven or eight, even nine pounds, when my son had weighed less than three. Infants who had entered the world with nervous systems fully developed and lungs that would breathe on their own. Those with hearts that would not forget to beat. All things my child would need two additional months to acquire as he lay incubating inside his box of glass.

But now his height measures up! His motor skills are sufficient!

His ability to converse is ample! And all his internal workings are performing up to speed. He is active. He is healthy. He is ready to go!

And I am at peace. Even as I look back on his birth I feel this way. My son is a fighter. A survivor. And this realization, this is profound, because a fighter is who he will continue to be. He will fight, even when we fear he has no fight left.

And too...for now, play-school begins! At our neighborhood community center we spend one hour twice a week in a sizeable room full of blocks and trucks and three-piece puzzles. This is Grant's first time enjoying himself alongside children his own age. I am introduced to women whose ages are akin to my own and following what seems a lifetime spent under "house arrest," the experience is nourishing.

As the weeks progress I begin to observe the other new mothers present. Most, I discern, are well acquainted with one another. I learn, in fact, that many have been socializing for a good amount of time. And this socialization has taken place every week of every month for over a year, the first time being when their infants were four months old.

I discover then there is something "out there," a program known as a PEPS Group, or rather a Program for Early Parental Support. Each woman would have learned of this program through attending a birthing class. As a result, when the time arrives these mothers are enough set-up to find one another.

As chance would have it, my child is one and a half years of age before I realize these groups had ever existed. Having never been part of a birthing class, the mothers of preemies are simply not informed.

But then...

One year later.

Parker is born! A "full-termer" weighing eight pounds, nine ounces! As he enters the world no one whisks him off; instead I see (immediately!) his thick black hair, one inch long, that is arrow-straight and explodes from his scalp in classic rocker style. He is beautiful! He is at once swaddled and placed into my arms, and I never, never want to let him go.

In order to ensure my second child will remain within me the entire eight and a half months (achieved!), I am advised to take precautions. My specialist, the on-call at every moment, high-risk pregnancy doctor, advises me that in order to compensate for my—here it comes...*incompetent cervix*!—I must receive stitches.

Although, I will not receive just any sort of stitches.

He will put in place his signature, no-playing-around style of stitches. The solid-shut, sewn-over-multiple-times, layered and layered, knotted-and-knotted again-and-again variety of stitches. The "gravity will not win" approach to stitches.

But that is the easy part.

Secondly, I will administer to myself twice weekly shots of Terbutaline in order to prevent any early and unwanted contractions. Contractions that may come about owing to my cervix (incompetent.) that might impatiently, and irrepressibly attempt to open before its time.

But again, that is the easy part.

He tells me I will lie in bed for six and a half months, rising once a week to travel to his office. This in order to further combat the merciless, omnipresent, never-once-taking-a-break gravity.

This then, is the "not so easy" part.

When I shower I must sit in a plastic chair…no standing. When I visit my doctor, having been driven there by anyone available, usually alternating shifts between my mother, my sister, and Robert, there is a wheelchair greeting me. And believe me, all this sitting is not beneficial to the ever-evolving appearance of my rear end.

Then, at around seven months, upon emerging from the hospital elevator, as my sister wheels me forward, a woman waiting to enter looks upward and sighs. When her eyes lower she glances at my sister and managing a significantly offended voice, begins to speak over my head. "Never would I have allowed someone to push me in a wheelchair simply for being pregnant." By this time hormones work well to keep me off-balance and, as a result, I allow her to witness my tears. But next the door shuts and, having passed judgment, she is on her way, smug, face motionless, eyes focused ahead, contentedly superior in every way.

At six months I witness a fallen stitch floating in the toilet and I panic. It is 9:00 in the evening and I make the call. My doctor's call-in (*on-call at every moment?*) partner phones me back within the hour. This is my first encounter with this man. He suggests I wait until morning and phone the office. But this man has never had a baby born at six months' gestation. He doesn't understand the uncompromising resolve to never have that experience again. And he has never encountered the "*I will now lift the semi off my child*" woman I have become at this very moment.

My mind is crystal and vibrant when I inform him, without uncertainty, that I am paying him a great deal of money to ensure I get the best care possible…in other words, sir…you work for me. He meets me at the hospital; well actually, after I arrive, I must wait another hour and a half for him to show up. (*It will be known to everyone everywhere that "he" is all-powerful, "he" is all-knowing*, that he, in fact, is "*the Almighty, himself*"). As he enters the room I am unmistakably not in his good graces. The tension is a tangible presence, and his eyes that never leave mine for what seems a lifespan reveal pure hatred. I don't submit and I don't look away.

But it was only moments earlier, while waiting in the empty hallway atop my gurney, when the nurse at my side had told me that, *because of me*, he, my doctor's *unduly inconvenienced* partner has unreasonably, has *needlessly!* been asked to leave a party. Despite my hormones, or maybe because of them, I look at the knowing smile on her face and we both explode into unmanageable, teary laughter.

My stitches are in fact loosening, many are already gone. Gravity, it seems, will persistently work its magic despite my constant prone position. I am wheeled into surgery where my livid doctor's partner re-stitches me.

So then, *Almighty One*, welcome to *my* never-to-be boring party.

❧

Following my six and a half months' interruption, as I lay prone in bed, I become weak, very. Once Parker comes home I spend as much time as attainable gradually coaxing back my strength. This I do primarily on weekends or as soon as Robert arrives home in the evenings. Of course this happens strictly on days when his work does not put him out of town. However, his out of town days are many…way too many. Since (appreciatively) he had stayed around throughout all my "high risk" worry, my period of non-activity, the time I gain sixty pounds, he must now fly about the country. He must make up for lost time without travel, the time during which he wasn't able to meet up with others face-to-face.

All the time, while having lain flat and incapable, we employ a live-in nanny for Grant, but now she must relocate back to Germany, and this relocation happens three days after I bring Parker home.

I am tired. The first three months I am up twice a night and then following that, I am up at 5:00 each morning. (My newest will not consider anything other than a 5:00 AM wake-up.) Robert helps with this when home, but too, he is also tired from too much travel, from baby, from our overly energized two-and-a-half-year-old. *I am weak*, my muscles having turned to pudding consistency from their all-too-lengthy interval without use. For the first time in my life I am overweight, a total of forty extra sluggish pounds on my five-foot-four frame after baby, placenta, and fluid are liberated. I get an infection at the site of my C-section incision. The medicine I take for this upsets my stomach. I develop a rash that covers my entire body, leaving isolated only my hands, my feet and my face, and this rash *itches. Enormously.* And no matter what topical cream I apply, no matter what medicine I ingest, these tiny-red-to-pustule-to-scab bumps covering the greater part of my body itch. for six *misery*-causing weeks. I produce too much milk. Despite my *large. Healthy. Full-termer*!

I have an overabundance of milk, more than he can consume. It gushes at inconvenient times…at the grocery, while sleeping. Quickly I learn to place a stack of towels underneath me at bedtime to avoid the extra burden of changing the sheets every middle of the night. And then, hadn't I been told that as long as you breast feed (and gush) you will not return to periods for the duration? It takes one month before I wake during the course of a much-needed slumber to a puddle of my milk mixed with a puddle of my blood.

We have a small corner grocery-café one block from our home. During my first attempt to walk (think amble) to this shop I progress half way up the block. Then I need a rest. This is not exaggeration, this is not embellishment…I amble (think waddle) half a block before I stop to lean against my neighbor's rockery…to catch my breath. I do not have a stroller to push, I am not traveling uphill. I'm not really "traveling" at all. *But I must pause then and there…in order to catch my breath.*

But it does follow that eventually, and ever-steadily, my C-section heals. I can un-curl my mid-section without pain or effort. I can lift my newborn without worry of injury to myself and the ability to move while standing upright finally comes to be.

It is at this point we hire a sitter who cares for my children two to three hours every afternoon for each and every weekday. During these hours I dedicate my time returning to pre-pregnancy energy and pre-pregnancy strength. As soon as nine months pass I am capable of running five to six miles, not slowing for hills, or puddles, or temperature. Not ducking out because of rain. I do this every day until my weight too is back to normal, until I can manage wholeheartedly my demanding, ever-consuming, never-to-completion, mother job.

I am grateful to this sitter who sticks by us throughout this difficult phase and, in doing so, helps to get us back on track. And later, as Grant enters, deepens, and continues in his life struggles, this same woman will again serve a crucial role in our family. She will be a dedicated ally to my son. We are immensely fortunate that she remains part of our lives to this day.

two

She Had Been A Tomboy

Pre-school has arrived and there is an afternoon when two new friends come to play. Grant is four. On this particular afternoon the three boys begin in the sandbox. There are dump trucks, "diggers," hand shovels (plastic). Holes are dug. Mounds are formed. And this construction activity, this lasts a bit. Maybe half an hour. Until trucks are hauled out of the box! And the four-foot tall yellow, blue, and orange slide is moved and placed in the sand. And the addition of this slide? Well this is *the* addition, *the* plaything that will define the day's purpose. In truth, this will offer up inspiration so as to transform the afternoon into a time like no other. Beyond remarkable. Really. Very. Remarkable. Due to this slide.

And, well, yes…the addition of water.

Barely an instant then passes before all thought sequence has progressed just so.

One of the three next locates the hose and, while doing so, all eyes light up in anticipation. The faucet is turned on and with encouragement the hose is placed and balanced at the top of the slide so that water spills freely downward. Cold water. Impatiently then the three take turns whizzing themselves to the bottom. They shove one another aside in order to cut in before their rightful turn. This since such a good idea this slide is, the chilly water is. Now breathless with laughter while covered in wet, cold sand, all in combination with the October chill, they continue to take turn after turn. And all this new fun? It ensues awhile, before one whisks the hose away and sprints to the treehouse. Now having reached this higher ground the hose-bearer can instantly crown himself "king" of the tree. And seizing his privilege as such, even fulfilling his duty as king, he proceeds to soak the others who, all the while, attempt desperately to dethrone him. But the water, this is turned on full power and therefore any effort at gaining ground proves futile. And, as anyone might imagine, this is the juncture when the noise level the three now generate has become as remarkable as the day itself.

And, as anyone might also imagine, this is the moment I am jolted into high alert.

I head outside to check on all the yelling, the shrieking, the odd sound of water as it soars beyond the two boys only to batter the side of the house.

The hose? This is turned off, by me. And at this time? Well, this is the moment all three realize they are really quite cold.

They are put in a warm shower (laughing), given dry clothes (pushing and shoving), and next hot chocolate is served. But not before having been given a long stern look (again by me). But despite the "*look*" (long and stern) which apparently is also really, very funny, the day is everything a four-year-old would want. In a word: remarkable.

It will be two decades later when "Grant" will tell me she had been a tomboy in her youth and that this type of play was her natural inclination.

I will learn only then that it was my *daughter* who had preferred trucks, Legos, and rocket ships over dresses, dolls, and tiaras. It was my *daughter* whose inclination was typically "rough and tumble male" in nature. It was my *daughter* who favored T-shirts and jeans.

My child who has the body of a boy...

He is my son. This is as clear as day.

And for still two decades moving forward she will remain hidden from me.

three

Children Are All the Same

The winter of Grant's pre-kindergarten year we look around for future schools. An elementary school for the year to follow is what we need. We decide then to look into a school designed for gifted children. We are given a scheduled "observation day" and we bring him to a classroom located on the main floor of a three-story building situated close to the university. After an initial meet and greet, the parents of the handful of four-year-olds present are directed to "disappear." There will be no outside coaching during observation hour! Robert and I find a coffee shop to wait out the time.

Throughout the classroom there are a variety of work stations that may intrigue the smart kids. The reading corner is one. An area assigned to advanced puzzle solving, mathematical gadgets, and scientific conundrums in another. Paint and musical instruments line a far wall. The young children spend this hour impressing, or not, the experts who observe and critique them. Placement into this exclusive school is not for everyone! The PhD specialists who have studied extensively the minds and behaviors of the gifted child flow from station to station in order to engage the children in their thought processes, the direction the children may take the projects in which they have begun to involve themselves.

Grant positions himself against a far-reaching wall. He is on his hands and knees seemingly searching for something, or perhaps, one may conclude, simply avoiding activities that truthfully he cannot manage.

As the hour passes Robert and I re-enter the classroom. We look around and then locate Grant against the un-utilized back wall. He is indeed crouched on all fours looking toward the ground and concentrating heartily. It is discernible that his task is all-consuming and, therefore, also understandable that he has not observed the adults who have returned. Robert goes to him, tells him it's time to leave. But the desire or the intention to leave is beyond him. He tells us he cannot abandon his work because it is not complete. He holds two dozen or so paperclips in his hands and is searching for more. The helicopter he plans to build will come to be after he has found enough. He cannot understand the notion of quitting when his goal is so very crucial and he is despondent as we exit the room. His quiet tears reflect this.

Later, that which is unforeseen comes to light as we learn Grant had not been approached, not once, during his sixty-minute testing period. Not one question, not one inquisitive glance. According to the experts boredom had quickly set in. "*His choice of time spent showed neither creativity nor desire for learning,*" we read later. "*His conduct…too indifferent.*"

Within a week the packet arrives. There are four levels of acceptance into this program. One for immediate approval and three indicating various tiers of waiting lists. Grant's name is not listed within a single column. "*If your child's name does not appear,*" printed on the final page, "*he or she has been denied access.*"

Period.

No second attempts.

No exceptions.

Criterion has been set, the *experts* have passed judgment. Our son is ill-equipped.

In undeniable opposition to their assessment: this regarding Grant's "*ill-equipped*" *problem*, along with his "*no desire to learn*" *dilemma*, throughout pre-school Grant's desire for knowledge is urgent.

Unlike most children his age, unlike *most people of any age*, he is, without exception, *avidly, unfailingly, impatiently* interested in *everything*. Absolutely, in all ways, *everything*. He wants to understand the world. He wants to understand beyond the world. His wish is to know "*all.*"

At age three, the "why" stage? The age when suddenly this question has become *the* central theme of any and of all days... Well, as regards Grant, there is no limit as to how often this question is asked, and there is no pausing until it has reached an utter, undeniable, unanswerable dead end. Period.

The universe is a frequent topic of conversation and he might ask, "What is beyond the universe?" But in keeping with too many of his questions, I disappoint: "Nothing."

"*Why?*"

"Because the universe is infinite."

"*Why?*"

"I don't know."

"*Why?*"

"Because no one knows."

"*Why?*"

"Because people are limited in their knowledge."

"*Why?*"

"Because the universe is immense, *infinite!* And therefore it is impossible for anyone to fully study it and, since no one can completely study it, there is no way for people to understand it."

"But what if people are wrong, what if it isn't infinite, what if there *is* something beyond the universe but no one knows because it's too big and people are limited in their knowledge?"

"I don't know."

"*Why?*"

He focuses on shape, Grant. On pattern. He takes time to explain…to me, to anyone nearby, that squares, of course, are not cubes. Circles are not balls. Never would a triangle be confused with a cone…and on it continues. He's interested in dimension, he considers the space which shapes occupy and the juxtapositions of varying shapes as they relate to one another. The negative spaces too, he understands, have shape. He wants you to *know* this, *hear* this, the truth about color, about shape and pattern. About three-dimensional shape as opposed to one and two dimensions. He spends hours cutting, taping, and next assembling sheets of construction paper all for the purpose of forming colorfully patterned paper sculptures. And these sculptures, they frame the windows, they adorn the tabletop, they wind around the banister. All of this, until the tired tape holding them in place loses strength.

Maybe he is five when his grandparents pass a new construction, a modern home nearly complete. Grant's comments concern the arc, or dome shape of the roof. "The dome is the strongest shape and the most resilient design for a roof," we are informed. "This is a good roof if there is a storm."

Who knew? Well, his grandfather, being a mathematician himself. I have to wonder, though, for the first time, why aren't all roofs arced? Especially in hurricane, tornado, or for that matter, any old windswept region?

I am astounded how often I learn from him.

The last week of pre-kindergarten soon arrives and Grant comes across an enticing idea. Fittingly, he takes the many newspapers we have saved up for the final day and rolls them tightly length-wise before taping them in place. Having cut down the newly-designed shaft, but leaving a foot or so intact, he spreads the tube out as long as possible without allowing the pages to separate. When complete, he holds onto the uncut end while the scored pieces reach upward toward the sky and fan out. The look is playful, Dr. Seuss in appearance, a sculpted paper "firework." He spends all week on this project making one for each student in his class, he includes one apiece for his two teachers.

The final day of school is warm. High spirits, a liveliness seemingly uncontainable pervades, defines the mood. And as the mass of four-year-olds run about without pause it becomes clear that all this energy is in fact just so…without containment. Later cake will be served. Ice cream has been brought in. Cheer, cheerful exuberance, these are the principal characteristics that express all and therefore as I aid Grant in carrying the bundles of paper "whatevers" inside the classroom, the excitement, as if possible, heightens still. Wild curiosity, ardent expectation, these are read on every young face. But then, unexpectedly, everything *does* become nearly still, as all focus is directed toward the unforeseen spectacle before them, the marvel of the paper explosions, the fact they are en route toward them. And so the exhilaration, which is swiftly bolstered by the other children who now surround him, swells in Grant too.

Immediately then, owing to the fireworks, the inspiration generated by them, and due to this ever-rising enthusiasm, the two instructors decide to move any pre-planned activities aside. Accommodating, and now genuinely motivated themselves, they direct the kids to form a line. Next, starting in the school's courtyard, the group moves along and throughout the streets of our neighborhood. In every sense they embody a pageant, Dr. Seuss in style. They laugh, the kids, and they stride with self-importance, all the while holding their eruptions toward the sky. Tall and proud, hoping all will see, they show off. The teachers flank the group, one on each end of the procession. There is a smile on every face.

That was a good day. That was a good year.

At our nearly one-hundred-year-old home, the former attic now serves as the third and top floor. This space has been opened wide and its expanse matches the footprint of the two stories underneath. Running lengthwise the ceiling rises twelve feet, and sloping outward on both sides from the center, the ceiling gradually lowers until it meets each opposite wall and comes to rest at a height of eight feet. Glass doors match up with the lowered ceiling on one of these walls which spread out onto a narrow deck. There is an expansive view here reaching outward toward Lake Union before coming to rest at the Seattle skyline, then, gathered inward, is as much south-facing light as comes available.

Slanting down from twelve feet in the opposite direction, the eight-foot ceiling connects with a wide sweep of open, deep shelving and generously-sized drawers; drawers that are commonly partway open, halfway shut, and from which their contents perpetually spill out or become crushed, or, more often, both simultaneously. The paint on these shelves is scratched and chipped, the shelves themselves house disorganized and tightly packed, often no longer wanted "*stuff.*" But all this jumbled messy confusion stems from vigorous, enduring, and whole-hearted use.

Our former attic is our kids' playroom.

There is an evening when Grant is five and Parker is three that Robert invites two men from work, along with their wives, to dinner at our home. This is the first time we have entertained this group and therefore, in the case they would like to have a look at the upper floors I gather the kids to help straighten out the playroom. Still, I leave a reasonable number of toys for them to pick up on their own. One of these couples has no children, the other has children much more grown up. These two have made the decision to not bring their kids along.

As the guests arrive it becomes immediately clear that one of the women (*who is a guest in my home*) isn't going to have a satisfactory evening. And it seems, for whatever reason, her problem reveals itself as hostility directed toward me. Alone. *Really?*

Therefore instantly, and of course understandably, she is someone with whom I do not want to engage in conversation. Ever. (*But here she is!*) She doesn't like me. Or she doesn't like herself. These complications can emerge as an equal but opposite force. At this point who really cares?

When it is discovered we share a mutual friend her look is one of surprise which quickly turns to resentment. Immediately then she makes known that this friend (this friend of *hers*)...well, she has been her friend for years on end, since childhood. And too, a best-of-friends ranking between them had been established ages ago. And so every bit of this "*mine alone* best-friend status" friend of hers, it seems this unfortunate problem between us? This serves to further decide her mood, this serves to further elevate her dislike of me.

As it happens, once dinner is over, our guests would, in fact, like to see the rest of the house, well except "my" woman who wants no knowledge or part of my unwarranted life. She follows along begrudgingly. (*But really, can't you just pout downstairs?*)

As we assemble in the playroom she notices the blocks are arranged in colorful harmony, a picture-perfect pattern, which is something Grant will instinctively do whenever asked to tidy them.

"My" woman then (*a woman who, only a minute ago, I fed!*) aims her eyes forward and in a voice bold and showy makes her announcement to the crowd: "Forcing a child to arrange toys in that way, in a fashion just to impress, is abusive."

Okay!

Apparently, it seems, she, on no occasion, has become aware that all children are not detailed prototypes of the original. She leaves the room. Contrary to the response Robert awaits from me I decide not to offer an explanation nor surrender my fury. But she has to go!

And now.

I impress even me.

four

Our Family is Whole (*Lucky*!)

Our house, located in the heart of the city is turn-of the century farm style. Built before central heating, there are holes cut in various locations on the ceiling throughout the main floor. This is the manner in which heat had reached the upper floors during the era it was built. Most of the holes are closed off as heat is added but we keep one for the history of it, and for the love. The opening is situated on the ceiling above the long table in our dining room and reaches upward as it cuts through the floor of Grant's bedroom. It is slightly rectangular in shape, approximately four by five inches with a depth of roughly a foot. We place Grant's bed in a way so as to cover our weird and beloved hole.

Yes, we entertain not too infrequently, usually dinners. Robert is often up for cooking. I'm good for set-up, clean-up and ice cream or pie. So when the time arrives to move toward the table, we already know what to expect; we have lived this ritual many times over.

Grant and Parker, ages six and four, station themselves under Grant's bed and above the hole. They have worked all day "in secret" attaching objects to string, the objects that, when the time arrives, will swing above our meal. So eventually hovering overhead come creepy crawlers, rubber sharks and spiders, or cut-out pictures of hideous, freaky who-knows-what. Often a small foot attached to a short leg will appear. The laughter upstairs is the "*can't catch your breath*" type and contagious to the adults below. This a bit less so when a filthy shirt or mud-encrusted sock appears to dangle from above. Eventually, though, they run out of impressive "show offs" and this is the time the note is lowered: *Mommy, can we have ice cream and pie?* Of course, as long as pajamas, brushing teeth, and sleep come next. My kids are best friends and every mother knows the truth inherent there: What on Earth could be better than that?

➴

The Fourth!
This is a day *we are lucky*!
Lake Union is located four blocks below our home and, as told, when peering directly across this lake to the south, the downtown skyline openly presents itself. Then, at nightfall, the numerous lit windows of the city provide a brilliance that inevitably demands attention. Two prominent hills preside over this lake from both the east and west sides and, from their crests downward, sit continuous rows of unobstructed houses. Then, from the shores themselves, houseboats line up in order to reach toward the water's center. So it is from all surrounding directions that there comes a view of the lake wide and graciously open.

On this day each year there is a festival that takes place at the park below. The day brings with it food booths, art displays, kids' games, face painting, sunbathing, and more. And then two hours before sunset arrives? A concert begins. The music skims the open lake, spans out and disperses its sound in all four directions, to all four communities. And next, as the sky darkens, the fireworks begin. The pyro-technicians work their magic from a barge that is placed in the center of the lake solely on this day of the year. The fireworks, which the city sponsors, have power. They are specialized and brilliantly choreographed. They are *the* event of the summer.

And they are close!

From our children's third-floor playroom deck it seems we can reach a simple arm's length in order to grab hold of the bursting flames. The playful "crackles" erupt next to (or possibly inside) our ears. The explosions are bright, loud, and they are thrilling. So it is not uncommon to hear our kids and their young cousins shriek as they sprint back from the balcony to escape the approaching explosives that overpower the sky and lunge hungrily toward them.

Happily, every year on this day we host a party, as do many, many of our neighbors. The streets throughout are lively and wildly beyond.

Then too, that which is added to all this excitement? The crowds. Swarms of people enter our neighborhood on this holiday each year, and these arriving bodies count in the multiple soaring hundreds or more!

The festival-goers spread out as they head down each street that runs north to south toward the lake. Our house is situated on a corner lot and therefore we too are "front and center" as the multitudes advance. Upon observing the throngs we spot holiday hats or T-shirts, miniature waving flags, fluttering wands that explode with glossy fringe or red, white, and blue pinwheels.

Many carry picnic cloths and baskets, they push strollers and shoulder-ride toddlers.

As the years progress, starting when Grant is five, and ending as soon as Parker reaches ten, there are many, many people who begin to choose the route which runs down our street. They have come to prefer it to any other.

And here is why...

We bake!

As if Christmas morning, *the* morning itself has arrived, it's get up and go by 6:00 AM! Grant and Parker sprint to the kitchen still in pajamas, their enthusiasm bursting. Both are single-mindedly keen on the mission ahead and so it is a half-beat as we begin.

As a rule we start with cookies: peanut butter, chocolate chip and oatmeal, both with and without nuts. (No raisins. Ever. My kids have laid the law!) Brownies are next (also with and without nuts). And then we progress to lemon bars, Parker's favorite. But the real people pleaser are the donuts, which, over the years, actually become famous as return customers spread the word. Therefore, in seizing the opportunity, we begin to make these donuts in abundance but, truthfully, there are never enough. They are our pride: light, airy but doughy, and while still warm, we roll them in sugar. They are the dictionary definition of "I want more, *pretty, pretty please*?" Not surprisingly the three of us sample our way through the morning with huge smiles. The kitchen is a mess but who really cares? On this day? Not even me.

We set the card table on the sidewalk around noon and spread a red and white checkered cloth over it. We stack paper cups for the lemonade and provide napkins for the baked goods. And next my children sell: twenty-five cents for each delicacy, making the one exception for the donuts which, over time, we deem worthy of double. And, as predicted, this cost inflation does not discourage a soul. People buy five and six at a time. Then, as soon as the donuts vanish, the donut holes are brought out and for these my kids charge a dime. Possibly two people pass before they too disappear.

Yes, we bake a lot of sweets so it is all the way until at least 4:00 PM when the last cookie, lemon bar, or drop of lemonade is gone.

And this is when my kids count the pot. On average they have made a little over one hundred dollars! Of course they won't allow their thoughts to wander toward the price of ingredients or time spent baking, but no adult would ever think to dampen the thrill by bringing that to light.

They divvy the profits, then each take a few dollars and sprint to the corner grocery to buy well-deserved ice cream, because on this day, sugar is allowed in decadent abundance.

For years and years this bake sale is the awaited entertainment for grandparents, aunts, uncles, and parents alike. And this is true for us as much as it is for my kids.

five

Boyish Endeavors

Grant straddles his first and second grades. He is nearly seven. We spend a day at Lake Washington with a friend of mine and her three boys. Her two oldest are similar in ages to my two and her third is one year younger than each of our second-borns. She and I sit in beach chairs on the sunbaked sand and the five boys have positioned themselves near the shoreline. They are wrestling (playfully?), tossing handfuls of wet sand at one another (good-naturedly?), destroying each other's sand creations (light-heartedly?). The boys are laughing...for now. We, the moms, are vigilant, comprehending, as we walk toward the chaos in order to begin the intervention process, hopeful to prevent the all-out combustion we both know is inevitable.

As we approach the water, the "games" indeed have begun to escalate (surprise!) and it is Grant and her second-born who continue their brawl. During the confusion I overhear the younger boy say to my son, "What *are* you, *a girl?*" I understand at once Grant isn't proving himself worthy of the struggle. He comes out of the tangle, out of the water, and sits next to me. He is distraught. He no longer wants to stay and "have fun." Very soon we leave.

It is later that same summer when he attends soccer camp at a local park. As predictable the space consists of open grassy fields; one area is arranged for baseball, another for soccer. There is a rust-colored, chalky, quarter-mile track spread out between the two fields. The week proves to be hot, unusually so. The boys are asked to do drills and calisthenics, and each are required to run two turns around the loop of the track. The camp lasts three hours each afternoon for one week.

On the second day of camp, when I arrive to gather Grant, I perceive the coach is displeased. As I step from my car he walks toward me and, when capturing my attention, stops. He turns then and points behind himself as he singles out the track. Facing me again he can see that I too look toward the sole child who is literally shuffling as he moves along his way. Grant has only begun his second turn around the course. The others, every last one, had finished the required two laps a reasonable twenty minutes prior. As soon as the coach sees that I understand he stares at the ground. He shakes his head. I am not the one who prompts his frustration per se. But as he lets out a sigh my heart sinks, my mind tries to protect myself, strains to insulate my body from emotion, but unavoidably emotion wins the inner battle. I understand that he judges me. He feels I need to get a grip on my parenting.

But, by the age Grant is now, I have learned with utter certainty that it is meaningless to challenge him. He simply will not do a thing, *anything*, that he has no desire to do. Ever. Period.

But then how would one force someone to run faster? Pleading? No. Bribing? No. Demanding? Nope. Threatening? Never. Consequences? Never ever. Not with my son. And what is most disturbing of all? I find this to be as infuriating as the coach. I call to him, my defiant, puzzling son. He shuffles over and without words we leave.

It is during the spring preceding this that he plays T-ball. I come to the games regularly, which proves to be an excruciating effort on my part. By the third game I bring along a magazine, but too, I pretend to give some attention to the game. Typically Grant is stationed in the outfield, although, while there, he seldom looks ahead toward the next play, or any play. He, in fact, doesn't bother to glance around at all. Balls roll past him. He's unaware they are close by and so doesn't run toward them. In place of his participation in the game he hunts for clover in the grass, he plucks the unusual stems, the uncommon few, those that show four leaves. He watches for advancing clouds, studies their ever-changing shapes. So it is not without reason the other kids, the coaches, and the parents alike, are bewildered, frustrated. Then for some, this frustration turns to anger. I try not to display my outward anguish over this. On occasion, I will give a baffled shrug, at times a wince. But as the weeks progress, some begin to openly glare in my direction, again they are annoyed with me for not "handling" my child properly. Most of these are fathers who are determined to generate a win from this forty-five-minute, Tuesday afternoon, six-year-old T-ball game. The stakes do appear high! As if the outcome may well portend the future success or failure of their child. (Major League? Ivy League?)

Weighty anguish exists within me despite all attempts to defend perspective. (*Breathe slowly, Sandra…breathe deeply.*) Regretfully my stress stems from the judgment of these parents, but too, it invades from the worry I feel over Grant's behavior. I question what this may indicate, this obliviousness to the sport, this disregard of others. I talk to him about the game. His answer? "I think I played as well as all the other kids, Mom." Part of me melts for him. Part of me shudders. A raw and fearful portion of me hurts, profoundly. Yet too, another piece, albeit a frail, fleeting and reserved slice of me, is amused.

My son is a four-leaf clover.

six

School Daze

It's time to look around for another school. Grant will soon be five and it's time for kindergarten. We chose then a school that is so "just let me be a little kid already" friendly that I almost want to go there myself, and he loves it. There is a visit day as opposed to an "observation hour." The kids play, explore classrooms, meet teachers and Grant is accepted right away.

The school, located in an old, nearly forgotten part of the city, is made up of three early twentieth century homes. The placement of these reconfigured homes, as they spread out on what was once three separate properties, make a zig-zag pattern. The surrounding land has become playgrounds that meander between and around the buildings and open out onto two open play yards. The grounds are blanketed in grass, bark, and fruit trees. There is a tree house, a vegetable garden, a large climbing rocket ship, and the open spaces serve as places to kick around a ball. Cool!

The director of this elementary school is a seasoned professional with over thirty-five years' credentials. She is smart, worldly and highly dedicated to both her administrative work as well as the achievements of "her" children. When it is discovered Parker has dyslexia she spends the entire summer following his first-grade year helping him recognize words despite the inversion that plays in his mind. As a result, when school begins in the fall, his reading is caught up and, in comparison to many students, even beyond. She *knows* how to teach. And her dedication for this summer's instruction? Free of charge.

Our much-loved director calls. This is a few days after Grant's visit. Her question? "Would you allow us to have your son skip kindergarten and move straight into first grade?" I consider this. Talk it through with Robert. We realize that, in an obvious way, this makes sense but Grant is young socially. Rarely does he surrender his attention to the behavioral nuances of others around him and, as such, he doesn't consistently "get it right." Based on our confidence in and high regard toward the director, however, we make the decision to go ahead.

First grade. The students study addition and subtraction. This takes place within the first week of fall. But before week's end the teacher wonders, had she misread his brilliance? Was it, in fact, something else she had seen in him? I'm called to conference.

"I believe remedial work in math will be required." This is what I am told. This is what I am confused, *astonished!* to hear will be the subject of this conference. "His reading and comprehension, these are impressive, far beyond elementary school level. In regard to math? He answers not one question. He occupies his half hour drawing pictures or poking holes in and around the lines where answers should be written in." I ask if I can help him find solutions.

He evades the question.

But it was only the evening beforehand when Grant had asked

me to create a problem comprised of digits in a row numbering twelve or fifteen across and then a similar number of rows leading down. Next he added all this up. His calculation was finished in a swift breath and his answer was correct. I ask the teacher, "Will you provide him more difficult math work rather than simpler?" By the end of the week he is placed two grades ahead for math.

By fourth, and then during fifth grade too, he is placed in a room by himself and given math work that is beyond that which the other students are capable. He is alone because there is no level higher than fifth grade at this school.

There are times, however, when the fifth-grade instructor will include Grant in the regular classroom. On one of these occasions the teacher passes out a quiz consisting of one substantial problem. The pre-instruction on this type of math had recently taken place for all students except Grant. After exams are returned, the teacher is pleased to discover that each student has answered the question correctly. But, as he comes to Grant's work, he is surprised to learn that his answer is different from any other. Based on knowledge of Grant's proficiency he reworks the problem himself. Grant's answer is correct.

By fourth grade he joins the fifth grade for science. The instructor reports "when Grant presents a question it is advanced, too abstract, for the other students to follow." And this advanced question asking, apparently this happens as routine. "Your son, he understands these concepts, he knows a lot about the subject, it seems intuitively he does this, and, as such, he is enthusiastic to know 'all.'" The teacher continues, "I am unable to pull the discussion in the direction his questions lead without alienating the others." He tells me he will place Grant in a room by himself where he will be given individualized work. Individualized tests.

I am quiet for a moment, I realize that all this braininess that has come to light over the years, this is all very positive but equally, I continue to worry over Grant's inopportunity to interact with his peers. Already I wonder, actually I know, he is falling behind regarding this, and I fear this "as now standard arrangement to separate him off" is surely to progress this falling behind yet further. "Is there another approach?" Mostly I ask this inwardly. But ultimately, as is true for the instructor, as well as the director, as is true for Robert, and for me, there is not a single solution anyone can think of.

This is then a moment I tell myself...or rather, I work to convince myself, that this separating him out, this won't be detrimental, not in the long run. And too, *it is his brilliance, this* is the reason he is separated out. *This* is something *positive. Sought.* Moreover, *his brilliance, this* is the pure and simple reason he is unique among other kids. And his being unique? Surely *this* is no cause for alarm.

I, as of yet, cannot see the whole picture.

To my relief, within days of our talk, the director makes the decision to move Grant down a grade for all subjects other than math and science. Because no, he cannot keep up socially among the older children. He can barely keep up with his peers. They supplement for him elevated work nevertheless.

In addition to his intelligence it seems he is wise, Grant. This surfaces as well. And when on a day the fifth-grade instructor asks the class, "Who thinks people who smoke are bad?" every child raises their hand, but Grant. The teacher then asks Grant what he thinks. "I don't think people who smoke are bad, I think they are doing something that is bad for them." Another boy then remarks, "My grandpa smokes and he's not bad." As a rule he advances the conversation.

There is an afternoon I ask Grant how things are going with the other kids at school. His answer? "I'm sixty-five percent included among them." He experiences the world as an equation. One day he will tell me he understands relationships as a calculation of a different sort, an abstract mathematical computation. Feelings too are weighed mathematically. I can't begin to wrap my head around this.

seven

He is Inquisitive, He is Obsessive, He is Obstinate, He is Frustrating, He is Busy

You are a mean mommy!

The note has been lowered. When I read this I try not to grin. I see he is serious, I get that his anger is real and I do not wish to ridicule. It's just…I can't shake the notion that he has no idea what a mean mommy truly is, and so I will listen again as he informs me for the millionth time that day that his forced "quiet time" equates to punishment that is both unusual and cruel.

However, as it so happens, I am tired. In fact, to be honest, my amusement over this comes much, much later because I am *really very tired*. Not simply from the "full speed on" reality of raising two children under the age of five, one who defies and challenges me at every opportunity (this same child who, when older, will declare definitively that he hates me and *will always hate me!*) but too, I've been up since 5:00, remember? Grant has been awake since 7:00.

While Parker takes his afternoon nap I crave to take advantage of my hiatus from all the activity, my very much needed (albeit fleeting) leave from active duty. So I lay down on the sofa in our living room. But our living room opens wide onto our dining room. The dining room where is situated our ceiling hole. The hole that is located below Grant's bed. The hole he now covers with his face as he lowers the note. The hole from where I can hear his arduous breathing due to his difficult but crucial effort. I am not quite asleep and I do what I absolutely know better than to do: I glance over. I spot the note. Then, unfortunately, I am curious, so I walk over knowing all the while I am feeding his sense of control over the circumstances, over me. But, ignoring what is in my best interest, I untangle the note from the string. The note on which he has written that I am a mean mommy followed by a deeply indented, decidedly manic exclamation point!

I look up, and I stare at this face that fills the hole. This four-year-old face that is indignant, angry, and insufferably serious and I know that my own expression reveals emotion that matches his very closely.

Despite my (*I am your superior, your mother, dammit!*) stare he doesn't let up. Again…it is impossible that my son will do anything that he has no interest in doing and then, infuriatingly (of damn-it-all course) vice-versa.

I will learn one day about his obstinance (*his unique degree of obstinance*). It will become clear only then that this behavior is as good as inborn in profoundly intelligent children. But since I am unaware of this inherent peculiarity, I believe…*no*, in fact, *I know* that I am inadequate. Cruelly, terrifyingly, I recognize that most often I am flat out failing at this mothering job and I reproach myself. Repeatedly I ask…*why don't I have the look that will freeze my child in his tracks?*

Moreover, since it is impossible for any one of us to imagine the severity of difficulties still to arise, I have not one notion how much more serious my challenges, my subsequent failures, will become.

But for now, Grant has a choice. He can decide to be quiet, leave *me* in quiet, until Parker wakes, and then be allowed to join his younger brother for his after quiet time snack, *or* he can continue to interrupt *my* quiet time and watch as Parker alone enjoys his snack. Period.

But this doesn't dissuade him.

Naturally.

What should be understood is, had I refused to take the note his next move would have been simple: merely increase the volume of his breathing or, what is more likely, begin to hum ever-loudly (down the hole). I am annoyingly acquainted with the futility of changing locations. Say I had moved my non-nap to my room? His "you need to see this *right now*" note would have been hastily and noisily stuffed under my bedroom door. Ever-evolving faint to voluble breathing would have then ensued. Dole out more severe consequences? I already know I'm beaten.

And I want to ask him, I want to scream at him! *Why can't you just listen? Why won't you behave? Why can't you simply cooperate…like others? Like Parker?*

And, *as for Parker?* The child that *does* listen? The child that *does* do as he is asked? *Does* cooperate? The child that incites not a bit of my worry? He is pressed to the background of my thoughts for those very reasons. And, as for now, he too has no idea how much more difficult the upward battle will become…for him.

Neither of us realizes there will come a day he will spill over with anger, *with hurt*, all due to my lack of attention.

But since I am overwhelmed with Grant, will continue to be overstretched in caring for Grant, and since Parker will remain in my mind as the child without complication, I will be unable to recognize my neglect. Years, even *decades*, will pass before I am able to see all the hurt I will have caused him.

With profound regret Grant is, and will be, my focus, my mystery, my ever-escalating concern. And my immersion with him will only intensify. Psychologists, psychiatrists, "healers" will ultimately be sought for difficulties still to arise: attention deficit disorder, anxiety disorder, bipolar disorder and most significantly, the immeasurable confusion surrounding his/her gender identity. And it is this last challenge, above all others, which will emerge the key reason in furthering his defiance, his unsettledness. His "otherness." Already at this age, even now inside his four-year-old self, he knows his brain and his body give him conflicting information, and he has no way of understanding what that means. Although what he does understand is that he doesn't fit with "others." And he hurts. And I can't help. And as his mother I hurt too.

But, as for this moment, and owing to his unsettledness, *his otherness*, his exasperating *stubbornness*, he prefers choice number two. It is every day prior to this one that, as soon as he is allowed his "freedom," the routine has been unchanging, he sprints to the kitchen anxious for his much awaited after-hiatus treat. In contrast to that behavior, however, today he refuses to reveal that any of it has ever mattered. Who really knows with this baffling, frustrating child of mine...maybe it hasn't?

Either way his choice remains firm. His preference is to keep me awake, to keep me engaged. *No second thoughts today!* Today (as in many, many...way too many...days to come) he is fixed to the game, the game of the power-struggle. The power-struggle game that every parenting book cautions you to avoid. The infamous power-struggle dance that my genius young child has already mastered. As for me? I will try my best to avoid letting on that this is daunting. (*Keep ahead of it, Sandra. De-escalate.*) But God knows better than anyone that I am exhausted, and that my physical exhaustion has now been exacerbated by emotional exhaustion.

And this is the way our lives will continue along during countless occasions going forward.

Therefore when soon after we take a trip to the mountains we, unsurprisingly, experience much of the same.

The week of our vacation turns out to be *cold, exceptionally cold*...so that during the warmest part of the coziest day the thermostat reads negative two. And, as for the snow itself? This is dry snow, too dry to roll a ball into a weapon or make a snowman, but Grant is determined, despite being advised of the futility of his plan, he is single-mindedly determined to make an igloo.

An igloo...

An igloo large enough to crawl inside.

An igloo molded from powder.

From the condo where we stay, he takes a steel mixing bowl from the kitchen and fills it with water from the tap. He has recruited Parker as his igloo-building helper. He convinces his very innocent little brother that it will be fun, and yes, Parker does have fun…in sub-zero temperatures making an igloo…for an hour, maybe two. I deliver warm food and hot chocolate from time to time, check their ever-progressing damp to soaking gloves. Trade them out for Robert's and mine despite the oversized sloppiness. I put the kids' gloves in the dryer for the next round and, at least for Grant, it goes on like this for hours. *Literally hours.*

And, without question, this is because he is unlike *any other kid*, in fact, this is because he is unlike *any other person, period!* That I have yet to encounter, and frankly, that I ever will. As other children would likely have moved on ages ago. Possibly pledged to continue this project the following day. Or, what is most probable, *quit altogether*. Grant will not abandon his work. Nope. Not my son. Instead he remains obsessed, he remains obstinate, he remains all of this while he remains busy.

Determinedly so. (*Albeit, impressively so…*)

And therefore, after dark, he still works.

In the end, and despite the continuous glove exchanges, his fingers nevertheless are a bit "iced up." But when done, nine hours later, there indeed has emerged an igloo large enough to sit inside, a dense block of ice, wetted snow now compact, frozen and airless that will survive the remaining weeks of winter and most of the following spring.

All due to his inquisitiveness, his obsessiveness, his obstinance and his busy. All due to the fact that each of these traits are routinely firing at once.

And therefore it only makes sense that all "this" eventually leads to *this…*

And every parent has seen "*this*," if only once.

The dance. The "I cannot possibly take a break to use the toilet" dance. Infuriatingly Grant takes this dance to the supreme, the *drive me literally mad* absolute limit and exasperating beyond. Short of gathering him up, him flailing in protest, or literally dragging him along the floor by any body part accessible, he refuses to inconvenience himself with the toilet. He denies urgency. And then, if somehow you manage the gigantic feat of matching him up with the bathroom, well...you can lead a horse to water...

There comes a morning he wakes with a fever, a high fever. Too high! At the pediatrician's I quickly learn I must get him to a hospital, now. Preferably hours ago! He has a urinary tract infection... *He has a urinary tract infection.*

He has a urinary tract infection because of "busy"! If I weren't so immensely frightened I would murder him on the spot. Cuff and drag me away immediately because I am going to kill my child this instant, kill him in view of our doctor, and yes, I will do so with neither regret nor meaningless self-reproach!

My adrenaline kicks in full when he becomes limp. He is seven while this takes place. His size is on par with any "full-termer" I've known and frankly on the taller range than most. At the hospital I must carry him from the parking lot under the hot sun grunting and sweating, Parker trailing behind. Once inside I find a stiff sofa, the upholstery of which is too firm, too rounded, too slippery; the depth of which is too narrow. I place him there alongside his five-year-old brother and pray he doesn't slide off.

I begin the check-in process. Paperwork ensues, questions about insurance, am I the child's primary guardian? "*Don't you need to take him back and hydrate him?*" No. Paperwork will be filed. Protocol will be followed.

At long last they wheel him back and lower his fever. They set him up with an IV and he sleeps. Visions of the newborn ICU creep in and linger around the edges of my mind. Parker scrambles onto the bed and lies down beside him. The hug lasts a good while until Parker too falls asleep. Still they are best friends.

He spends a full week in the hospital. I sleep next to him on a rolled-out cot. I check his breathing. I feel his forehead. As I sleep the ICU enters my mind in its entirety. I wake with the memories of my tiny, fragile infant. I think about his small glass box. Inevitably I wipe away tears.

It will feel abrupt one day, already too soon, when he will abandon his obsession with *busy*. His interest in everything will wane, before dying away altogether. These changes will come as soon as all the trouble begins.

Yet, there is an afternoon during the early part of that future time when busy *does* circle back. Even if fleetingly.

And it arrives on a warm, late spring afternoon while in seventh grade. His science teacher has decided to take his students outside the classroom. The group heads to a saltwater beach nearby where the students disperse and explore. It is minutes after this "dispersing" then, when Grant catches sight of a large spray of water that shoots skyward from the cool, water-soaked sand in low tide. Now, if someone has never seen a geoduck, or better, one that is in the process of shooting downward from the near surface, then they do not have a proper vision of its size, its swiftness and its strength. This is not your run of the mill "clam". This is one *enormous* creature that, when fully grown and used to make chowder will likely feed eight, maybe ten people...possibly more. And this geoduck, this is full-sized. A big *clam*!

And a prize when caught.

This is where I'm uncertain but, based on prior experience, Grant likely has it in his mind to bring this enormous creature home to do just that. Make chowder.

He begins his frantic dig. No shovel. No, he just goes at it with his hands, full-strength. As it happens the geoduck is still enough near the surface that he is able to grab hold of its neck. But this geoduck is *strong, very strong*. Therefore he is unable to dig and hold at the same time. He calls down the beach for help but there is no one close enough to hear. *And he has to have this geoduck.* He continues at his endeavor; *he will not, under any circumstances, let go*!

As the hour comes to an end the students are asked to reassemble on the bus. The teacher makes the head count. One is missing. He leaves the bus to look down the beach. And there he is! My son. He calls to Grant but Grant refuses to let go of his treasure. He refuses to get on the bus! The teacher must then walk down into the low-tide mess and gather him up! (God help me.)

On the bus Grant is visibly disheartened.

The students are late to arrive back.

All are tardy for their next class.

Because of him.

When I learn of this I feel I am back watching six-year-old T-ball, or rather, looking on as a lone child shuffles his way around a track.

eight

Sometimes the Universe Plays Fair

Our beloved babysitter along with her family host an ornament party each December. Every participant (only women) bring three Christmas baubles to the game. Dice are passed along in succession and, when lucky enough to roll a seven or an eleven, the recipient is given permission to choose one of the colorfully wrapped packages displayed on the low table that is the midpoint of the circle we have formed. Advancing with the game, the next lucky roller can either steal away an ornament that had been previously unwrapped or choose an unopened one from the stash. Subsequently the game progresses like so until each ornament has been chosen or stolen. (Stolen a maximum of three times!) Competition can be fierce, think cut-throat, and because of this there is continuous laughter as we all observe our ridiculous, childish behavior.

The winter Grant and Parker are four and two, our sitter asks the other women if "her" two little boys can join the all-female gathering and, as it happens, my sons are unanimously welcome. This one time.

Enthusiasm overcomes as Grant and Parker anticipate the party, since, any chance to be with their sitter is awaited just so.

Once there, however, and despite their very young minds being "aware" of the rules, it is as soon as the warring has begun that they become confused, say even distraught. The notion that someone can freely take a treasure (that belongs to *them)* away? (and then keep it?) is nothing short of baffling. (Doesn't that contradict everything they have been taught?) And this injustice is especially true for my very passionate, extremely sensitive, oldest.

When the time comes for Grant to open his first package, he is, let's just say, *eager.* Hastily he rips into it. Then, as soon as he has taken his initial glance (clearly with satisfaction), he proudly holds up his prize for display…part of the rules… Immediately then there are ardent *oohs* and *ahhs* from all around the now covetous crowd. Plainly this is *the* ornament of the day and immense delight over his newly acquired gem (a delight further enhanced by the grownups' adoration) along with a deep sense of possession fills him. He's forgotten it's up for grabs.

Not unexpectantly it is simply the next turn when it is taken from him. After which his expression reveals both alarm and then outward panic that is heartbreakingly innocent. Subsequently then, as if never enough, it is only the turn following when it is snatched up and lifted away again. His mind spins; there are a few tears but this appears unnoticed by the zealous adults in the room and, as a result, the "fun" continues without indecision, without hesitation. I roll the dice next praying I will be put in position to retrieve the beautifully painted Santa in the shape of a five-point star from the latest offender. But I fail… Since an ornament can be passed only three times before it is out of play, my anxiety builds.

But then, remarkably, say unbelievably, the very next person to roll a seven or an eleven, after passing over five other players, is Grant! He jumps up. He runs around the low table and seizes his Santa. He holds it tightly to his chest as if to say, "No more." His smile is enormous. It is *rightfully* and *forever his* prize.

Grant remembers this game with fondness, as if a better time could not be imagined. If ever invited back, and this is true to this very day, he would be the first to arrive and the last to leave.

And so, it is that sometimes, even in the simplest ways, an incident will turn out to be just, all the more gracious and compassionate.

This ornament will be my child's treasure permanently. As for me, it will be something more, vastly so. It will be a memory to grasp ever-firmly and hold passionately close, because this star marks for me a day when the universe decided to play fair with my child.

nine

He is One
Who Makes it All Look Easy

There is an afternoon when a handful of graduate students from the University of Washington pay a visit to the pre-kindergarten class Parker attends. He is four while this takes place. The older students seek children who will participate in a study that will assess the way in which temperament plays a part in future successes or failures. The study follows the children over the course of three years. The research will take place within a controlled environment at the university five to six times per calendar year.

The children are promised a gift at the end of each session and, because of this, Parker is interested, *eager*. in fact. Routinely then, from the assortment of choices, he selects a stuffed animal, always a stuffed animal (his collection already far from miniscule). He is thrilled with his rewards and looks forward to his sessions with enthusiasm.

There is a day he is asked to sit at a small desk for twenty minutes. There has been a bowl of candies placed on this desk and there are blocks, puzzles, trucks, among other toys scattered out of reach throughout the room. Parker is instructed to not leave his seat and to not eat any candy for the twenty-minutes duration. As told to him by the research team, he will be given the bowl of candy and can play with the toys after the twenty minutes are up, as long as he conforms to these guidelines. If, on the other hand, he leaves his seat or eats any of the candy before the required twenty-minute period, no candy will be allowed and he will not be granted the remaining ten minutes to play with the toys spread about. The usual afore-promised post session gift, however, is his to keep.

I sit with the research team behind an oversized one-way mirror and, alongside them, I watch my son. Ten minutes pass. Fifteen minutes go by. At this point one of the graduate students confides, "Not one four-year-old tested thus far has held out this long." Parker stares at the toys, he fingers the wrapped candies, but, it is evident he keeps mindful of the two contrasting outcomes that will arise from compliance or lack thereof. He controls himself, his desires, for the five remaining minutes. As I leave to enter the room where he waits one of the researchers stops me. "Your son will grow up with remarkable success," she says. His temperament, it seems, is well-suited for accomplishment. And, as told to me that very day, this becomes the absolute, undeniable truth.

Later, when alone, I take a moment to allow in a thought, a welcomed thought. I consider then that…perhaps, just possibly? I may be doing something right…with this child.

-❧

School *Days*…

Throughout elementary school, the children are given fifteen minutes of early morning runaround time before the bell will call them inside.

As for Parker, by third grade, during this quarter hour, a ritual among he and his friends has long been established.

Routinely then, as our car pulls up, we spot three boys lined in a row who balance both feet on the lower inside rung of the wooden fence surrounding school property. They are stretching up and over this fence, armpits hooked across its top. They have positioned themselves on this lookout for the sole purpose of eyeing our car, for the sole purpose of catching a glimpse of Parker. As our car stops, we hear rhythmic pounding, which is definitely keyed-up and escalating still. The playground fence is where, and on which, they pound. I listen as they chant Parker's name in ever strengthening volume, over and over.

As he exits the car the boys jump to the ground. They surround him, excitedly, impatiently. Immediately there is playful jostling and jubilant laughing. They joke and they tease as they urge him toward the playground. This is then, the inter-changeable ritual and commotion they generate, the four boys, as they run off, in order to run around.

Parker mixes, mingles and he joins. He is not sixty-five percent included. This kid, he is all in.

Additionally, it is already by grade-school that Parker has disciplined himself to study hard. Therefore by middle school, and then during high-school too he is organized, his assignments are thorough. Reliably he hands his work over on time, when extra credit is optional, he eagerly fulfills. His grades are impeccable, stellar. All A's consistently.

And he is kind, Parker. He is respected; his keen sense of humor, I'm told by his teachers, matches his brother's unerringly. As he advances in grades he is asked by the school psychologist to mentor younger kids, those who struggle socially.

He is asked to birthday celebrations; he's invited on vacations with friends and their families. The girls search for him at school dances. He seeks and is sought by all kinds: those younger, older, his teachers. He qualifies for advanced classes in all subjects. Willingly he accepts the additional challenge. He involves himself in extracurricular activities: school plays, track and field; he joins a group of student beekeepers who make honey and store their hives on the rooftop of the school.

When high school arrives he alone forms an environmental club. He recruits many to the effort. He wins a statewide achievement award for his accomplishments and for the environmental awareness he has brought to others. He attends outside school trips and expeditions; one takes him to Africa where students and faculty install computers and offer technical training to impoverished regions. He twice travels to the Arctic Circle where he spends three weeks camping, kayaking, and studying geology.

One day he tells me he plans to attend the best college in the nation. One day he will receive his PhD from a school that, many times over, has been rated the number-one college in the world.

ten

Always, Always, Always There is Something, Always...

Not without cause I feel that drama hovers about my oldest child.

In truth, I believe it pursues him, and I believe it does so adamantly, effectively and continuously. And then too, by way of being his mother, this "forever-hovering about drama" doggedly shadows me as well.

He has his six-year check-up. In three days' time, when results are back from the lab, I get a call. It is a Friday at 5:00 at the start of a three-day weekend, and the pediatrician leaves her message. "Will you please give my office a call? There is something wrong with Grant's blood."

Yes. This is a message I receive at 5:00 PM at the start of a three-day weekend. As such there will be no office to call short of Tuesday.

And there is more.

I listen to this message immediately after I have come to a dead stop in the parking lot behind our neighborhood video store.

I continue listening as I walk into the video store to inform the employees that the rear axle has fallen from my car and therefore the car can go neither forward nor backward. I finish listening as I walk with the manager of the video store back out to look at my car which sits diagonally across the narrow parking lot blocking both the way into the lot, and the way out of the lot. I finish listening as I stand with my two children inside the foyer of the store to escape the rain that has now begun, the foyer where other Friday evening potential movie watchers (aplenty) must pass before noticing they are going nowhere.

Because of me.

Cross my heart.

And all this "wrong blood news," this "no office to call predicament," this goes on while I wait for the tow truck, which will arrive to rescue my car between one and one and a half-hours out.

I would phone Robert to assist with either the car or the kids or the doctor but he has gone fishing. Literally. In addition, he has gone to a remote area where there is no cell phone reception. In fact, where he and his friends fish, there are no phones available, period.

I call the doctor's office. She will be out of the office until Tuesday, the automated response informs. "If you feel this is an emergency, please call 911."

Our pediatrician has left her message, and I have received her message. She knows this will be the case. She has told me that there is something *wrong* with my son's *blood* and she will be *out of the office*, in fact *she will be unreachable*...for three days' time.

I dial the afterhours number. A doctor who is not a partner with my doctor phones me back. He will be my doctor for this phone call because both doctors associated with my doctor will be unreachable. Until Tuesday. This doctor has been given no heads up that I may call. He has no chart, no lab results and no history of, or with, my child. He tells me he will look into the matter.

He wonders whether there is something in particular I expect to collect from the report. I step enough distance from the foyer to prevent my young children overhearing and I tell the doctor of the full blood transfusion my son had received as a pre-term infant.

He assures me that blood donated to newborns is screened against impurities far beyond that of any other blood stored. He pledges it is kept in separate banks so as to never be confused with blood given to the general population.

I feel a surge of nausea despite this doctor's would-be-calming affirmations and I ask the questions I do not want to ask, the questions to which I already know the answers. "Yes," he responds. "Errors have arisen, impurities have slipped through but these are rare occurrences." And... "Yes, it is possible but, again extremely slight, that a problem arising from tainted blood would emerge six years later."

This doctor is kind, he is sincere and he is patient. But too, this doctor, he has no clear account of my son. He doesn't know that his entire young life has been a series of rare occurrences and extremely slight possibilities and therefore I am certain he would not understand when I now rush to the restroom in order to relieve myself of my nausea.

I stand for a few minutes next. Motionless, head down, before raising my eyes to stare into the mirror. And I ask myself then... Why incessantly Grant? Why the crises surrounding him...always? Hounding him...continuously? I wash my mouth. I breathe. I splash water over my face before looking down again. And I fix my eyes just there, as if the answer lies somewhere in the tile.

An hour and forty-five-minutes pass in the foyer before the tow truck arrives. Purposely I avoid looking at the waiting crowd eager to rush to their cars. I simply stand with my children focusing on our car, eager for it to be fastened down. I envision the three of us at home. But contrary to what I imagine, my children and I cannot secure a ride in the truck's cab. This, I'm informed, is company policy. "I am sorry," says the driver, and I can see that truly he is.

I take my two sons by the hand and we begin the six- and four-year-old short-legged walk in the evening rain the eight blocks home, the raindrops masking my teary worries and concealing my escalating fear.

Once home my now-doctor phones me. He has hunted down the report. He takes a deep breath and pauses before, in a somber voice, tells me my son has contracted hepatitis B. His blood sample shows this. There is another interval of silence that follows. Then I speak. "What does this mean? Is it serious?"

His answer. "Hepatitis B is serious, very. Particularly in children." He pauses. Then, as if an afterthought, he says, "Hepatitis B is detected in donors' blood easily. It would not have been passed through transfusion." In other words, my son's premature birth does not factor into the equation. It is something other.

It is, I learn, an infection transmitted through semen, vaginal fluid, and of course, blood. Nearly one hundred percent of those infected contract it by the use of dirty needles or unprotected sex. It causes irreparable damage to the liver, most likely to be

severest in children. More often than not it will lead to death…
in young bodies. Currently there is no treatment to prevent this.

Dirty needles? Unprotected sex? Death?

Practical joke?

Nightmare?

Suddenly deprived of oxygen and stripped of my surroundings I spin. I can find neither air nor words. My body is frozen, non-existent, emotionless.

Both my parents are with me within the hour. We sit. We look for symptoms that can take four to six weeks to appear.

Abdominal pain… No.

Dark urine… No.

Fever… No.

Joint pain… No.

Loss of appetite… Never.

Nausea and vomiting… Not yet.

Weakness and fatigue… Can't detect it.

Yellowing of skin and the whites of eyes… Cheeks rosy, eyes sparkle.

Again I call my now-doctor.

This I do despite, at present, I am a mother who takes pleasure in shooting her young son's veins with heroin before sending him off to wherever one would send a six-year-old to become a sex slave.

I call.

Can we administer the test again? We can. On Tuesday.

So I am raw, raw and sluggish. And it is a lingering, restless six days, three before the blood draw, three for the report to return, before I am informed that the lab had mistaken my son's blood with that of another patient.

An instant doesn't pass before I avow our AWOL doctor will no longer be our doctor.

eleven

Confusion
Begins for Real

G rant is close to me, too close! My therapist tells me this. It is time for him to bond with his father. "This is appropriate and, moreover, it is necessary (crucial!) for proper development when a boy is eight."

The guilt begins. What have I been thinking? He accompanies me everywhere. I drive him to school and I bring him back. He goes to the playground and I am there. We ride bikes. We read books. We go to movies and plays. He loves the Museum of Science, the Museum of Art, the Museum of History, where I take him. We swim. I (attempt to) teach him tennis. We hike.

Except, as all this goes on he becomes increasingly angry with me.

But too, he needs me. Desperately. He clings. I find the depth of his neediness the thing that is most baffling, most concerning. And these extreme moods, they seem to be wholly arbitrary, therefore I am unable to anticipate the swing. I struggle to hug him and I struggle to talk with him. He cries and he yells. He acts out when others are around so that my attention will be directed solely with him. I am confronted with myself, my ineptitude.

Again I realize we wouldn't be here if only I had done things right. He begins to fight with his brother. I am now confused about the best way to be his mother and how to pass him off to his father. It seems there is nothing instinctual that will guide me, not a thing that will lift me from the immense burden of my failure. I am filled, *saturated* with the heaviness of my failure. And my guilt. I am the cause of this. I have neglected to understand that he must bond closely with his father now that he is eight.

Once a week then Robert takes Grant to dinner. They talk "guy" stuff. On the weekends they assemble and launch rockets. They take bike rides. They join a father/son group called Indian Guides. They join Cub Scouts where Robert helps him make a pinewood derby car which they enter into the annual Pinewood Derby Race.

They do all this while bonding. As their bonding ensues throughout these various activities, however, Grant asks about me: "What do you think Mom is doing right now?" He rushes to me as he arrives home. Robert and I are bewildered as to what to try next. My guilt increases. My confusion is infinite.

By age nine, ten, and still later, there continues to be long, emotional months during which Robert and I attempt to "pass him over." But we fail. And it seems the harder we press, the less ground we gain. And all the while this goes on, his need of me grows increasingly urgent, as if his very survival depends on a continuous, never-taking-a-breath immersion with me. His anger too surges. He provokes, he spurs, he incites, he goads, he presses; he does this every day. He does this toward me. And then there is the flipside, over and excess and above and always, I am the one he runs to for comfort. Unceasingly.

And all mixed-up with these fluctuating temperaments is his desire for my approval. He is frantic for my approval. Through the miasma of his anger, however, I don't yet realize this. But it is *just that*, *my approval*, his want of it, that will be the cause of his ever-mounting resentment toward me. Then, added to all this confusion is a *hatred* of himself for wanting it. It is a hatred of *me* for his wanting it. And all this anger, anguish and uncertainty, it will manifest as hostility, antagonism, and defiance, both profound and devastating.

This is our future.

And *every bit* and *every day* of this emotional havoc will do no other than devour the both of us. Steadily, ever gradually, piece by excruciating piece.

And as I will continue to have no knowledge of "his" true identity, as I will be unaware of the range of additional challenges still ahead, I simply ask myself, I plead with no one, when will he grow to be less worrisome? Less problematic? No longer all-consuming? When?

The answer, of course, lies nowhere.

And over the years, as the vast array of challenges do emerge, the answer will continue to lie nowhere. I will watch as his entire existence bends to the debilitating phobias, incapacitating anxiety, and profound depression that will conquer him entirely. And these challenges, they will only strengthen his need of me many fold. And as I will carry on, discouragingly on, in the dark, and since his suffering will continue to surface primarily as anger, the *real* battles will begin: the endless power struggles, an ever-rising intensity to them, his swelling hatred of me; his incessant days, months, even years of laying prone.

And it will be just that—his unremitting motionlessness, both emotional and physical—that is the reason I will position myself in the doorway of his bedroom over and over, begging him, pleading with him to *do something*. And I will linger there, him staring off and away, while I ask him, "Please tell me what is wrong." But as he himself will be unable to fully understand his anguish, his answer each time will be the same: "I don't know." He is stuck, and throughout too many years to come, as other kids continue moving forward, he will remain just so.

Inescapably then alongside his anxiety will be my anxiety. Together with his depression will be my own. Futility, we'll share this too. And all this heartbreak, this emotional pandemonium, this will continue throughout puberty and significantly beyond.

All this, despite hours and hours, during years added to years of seeking help. Help for him, as well as for myself.

A mother is only as happy as her unhappiest child. I have come to understand this at my core. And I will continue to know this in its most stark and pure sense year after agonizing year moving forward.

Eventually there will come a day, unavoidably a day, that we will both reach an emotional breaking point. This then will be the time all this exhaustion, uncertainty, every bit of this anger and despair will threaten to tear us apart.

But I don't see it coming.

And I don't know how to prevent it.

And I will continue to fail.

And where is Parker during all this mess? This hopeless,

uninterrupted concentration on Grant? When will I give *him* his rightful time? How will I do this alongside Grant's insistent need of me? His unremitting and devastating falling apart in front of me?

How? When?

How…

Painfully, as time advances, Parker will be shoved further and further to the background of my thoughts, of my concern. *I* will shove him there. *I* am guilty of this. And it will only grow more and more punishing as my neglect will go on and miserably on. Too many years will have elapsed before I will understand that Parker hurts immensely, overwhelmingly. Too many years will pass before I realize that, in simply being the trouble-free child, Parker will suffer, that he will be "punished" for his cooperation and for his patience. Too much time before I will understand that *both* my children hurt. *Both* suffer…both need me, in dissimilar ways yes, but equally.

Although, for now, as I am continuously wandering about in a fog of confusion, I am unable to see. I don't see Parker's pain; I am incapable of detecting the imbalance. My worry over Grant obscures all other.

Inevitably then, a day will arrive, when it will be just that— my persistent over-attention of Grant alongside my continuous under-attention of Parker—that will threaten to tear our entire family apart.

And I can't stop this any more than I can stop the other.

Because I don't see…

twelve

Parker

Parker's fifth birthday. We invite classmates, neighbor kids, and family to the party. I craft a large sign and hang it above the dining table: *Parker is 5*!

We hold the celebration on a Saturday so Robert can be present. He loves construction equipment, Parker does. Diggers, drillers, scoopers or anything along that spectrum. (This following an elongated dinosaur phase, this in addition to his beloved stuffed animal collection.)

We play pin the bucket on the digger. The board, the pieces, I have made them myself. He receives toy trucks, aplenty. This from us, from grandparents. Cousins. Hot dogs are served before the cake, the ice cream. Then, it's time to pass out the party gift bags and eagerly the kids tear in. I have placed a wooden airplane kit in each bag and straight away the kids want help with the assembling.

It is at this point that Robert turns toward the boy who sits beside him. And to this boy he offers his help.

But Parker, already on his way to Robert, sees all this, this offer of help. To a boy. Other than himself. Immediately then he feels the searing injustice of it. He lowers his head. And, although he now realizes he is second in line, he goes over to where Robert is and sits close by, touching him. There are no tears during the party.

These will come later.

Nevertheless it is his behavior that speaks all that is necessary, it says: "This is *my* dad." With eyes downcast, this voices, "Why is it always someone else's turn before mine? Just like with Grant? Why not me? Why can't I sit on Dad's lap while he helps *me*?"

"Why don't you care about *me*, Dad?"

Excruciatingly, it says this as well.

In all his young innocence, he is not fully aware of the reason for his anguish. At this time, we too are unable to understand the cause for the strength of what he feels.

But what I do come to realize later, *what I come to realize too late*, is that this is due to the unremitting focus I direct toward Grant. Grant's desperation continuously draws my attention away from *anything or anyone* other than him. And now Parker feels forgotten by Robert as well. And this pain over his father, that is combined with my never-pausing attention on Grant, this devastates.

But I don't understand. Still, I cannot see that Parker's need of me is as urgent as Grant's.

Cruelly, this childhood injury is a burden Parker will carry with him for the rest of his life. And undeniably, as I am the cause, this is a burden I will carry for the rest of my own.

And, a year earlier when I arrange his dinosaur party the outcome is much the same.

This is when Parker turns four.

I spend weeks (literally) making "dinosaur eggs" crafted out of papier-mâché. I immerse strips of cloth into the plaster I have mixed for this purpose. When the strips are wet (and messy and sticky), I wrap them around medium-size balloons. Then, once the plaster dries, I remove the balloon and fill the "eggs" with candy and small gifts. There is, of course, one for each child.

I have devised a scavenger hunt, a "dinosaur egg" hunt, which will take the kids throughout the house and around the yard, eventually coming to end at the sandbox, where the eggs have been partially buried.

The eight or so kids take off, race against one another. They stumble and hurriedly get back up. "Slow down!" This shouted by me, to no effect.

Eventually each arrives at the sandbox where, with some pushing and with some shoving, they dig out the colorfully painted, partially buried giant eggs. Immediately then, all faces illuminate as hastily they gather up and break open their treasures.

The scene is *awesome*!

This is what I think.

It is once all guests have left when Parker tells me he has never had a fun birthday.

…The focus on Grant, my worry over him. All this at Parker's expense. Confusion and fog, fog and confusion. This is my entire range.

And it will not end, Parker's pain. Sorely the emotional damage caused by years of being the child who *has it all together* cannot be taken back. Ever. And when on a trip during graduate school, this hurt only resurfaces to remind the two of us again.

We meet up with Parker in the mountains of Oregon, Robert

and me. He is twenty-five. The lodge where we stay is a stunning, works progress-era, log mountain retreat. Timberline.

Despite it being May, skiing is just outside the door. There is an outdoor pool, a hot tub. And there is wide-open sun. There is history at this lodge and full display of it. And naturally there is a restaurant. A comfortable, wildly cozy, log-enclosed, fireplace-lit dining room.

After our meal dessert is brought out with a candle and, once more, I feel, *I believe*, everything is perfect.

After dinner Parker reproaches me for not having brought a dessert from home, one that I had taken the effort and the time to make personally.

The searing wound felt by the child *who makes it all look easy*.

thirteen

Grant

Although Grant's need consumes and weakens me, his need disposes of him with more callous determination still. It permeates him everywhere—his essence, his mind, his soul—so that nothing of his person is left untouched. Nothing of him is left uninjured.

Terrifyingly an understanding of his despair is out of anyone's reach. His desperation is, in every single baffling respect, utterly undefinable. (Who, please, can help me figure this out? Where is that person who can help *him*? Enlighten *me*?)

But, as if the world itself has an insatiable need to shatter our spirits, as if there will be no balance in the universe until our wills are irreparably broken, it becomes increasingly implicit that our suffering will remain without solution.

It is eventual, and distressingly overdue, when Grant will tell me about his inconsolable need of me, his resentment toward me. But this won't happen until fourteen additional years have passed. Only then will I learn that it stems from his awareness that I refuse to "see" him. Selfishly I will not peer deeply enough. He is both enraged and entirely heartbroken that I deny the truth of him, that I refuse to recognize the entire picture *of him*. ("I present myself in front of you every day, Mom, I am trying to show you that I am broken. Why can't you see me? Why won't you help me?") I am his mother, his very own mother, and it is unforgivable that I don't even know who he is.

At ten he begins his retreat from the world. Computers become his escape, his solace, His teachers urge him "join the other kids outdoors," this during morning recess, lunch break. But he ignores their well-meaning appeals. He will continue to sequester himself and he will concentrate fully on the screen before him. It is only through staying out of view that no one will look at him, and not see him.

The teachers describe to me his behavior: "Something has changed, he is out-of-sorts. He withdraws but then in absolute contrast he shouts out answers at times inappropriate. It's as if there are no others in the room to consider. He's not focused. He can't sit still. It appears as if he lives a world apart."

"Will you please work with him?" It is then our director who intervenes; it is she who asks this question of me.

She considers that I have neglected to set proper limits with him. She suggests I begin to do so.

(*Put your child on track now, Sandra!*)

But I don't understand *how*…

Inevitably then, when middle school arrives, a time when conformity is everything, a time when conformity is the *only* thing, it will be this erratic, unsettled behavior that will inescapably mark him a target of ridicule.

fourteen

An End Approaches
A Beginning Looms

We pay a visit to the middle school Grant will ultimately attend, this during a time when the school's doors are open to prospective families. As assigned in the evening's program, the kids move from classroom to classroom. In every room there is a different subject. For each they spend twenty minutes.

Grant is early to arrive in the first classroom, mathematics. The instructor engages his sole student in playful numbers games. Grant is quick to his answers. The teacher alters his approach. He veers toward advanced math, steadily increasing the difficulty. Grant is quick to his answers. Grant next begins to ask the teacher questions, ever-challenging, manifestly "adult" questions. During the ten minutes the two take turns asking and answering, both engaging enthusiastically.

Not surprisingly then Grant feels comfortable at this school. Not surprisingly he is accepted right away.

The final day of elementary school soon arrives. Every grade has free play all afternoon and a potluck picnic is furnished by the parents. It is early June. The weather is warm, inviting with the absence of wind. Tablecloths lie still, hair keeps neatly out of eyes, paper cups stand upright. The mood is relaxed.

Although in comparison to this tranquil setting there is, of course, the wild, say frenzied, enthusiasm of kids in anticipation of summer break freedom. Water guns (undersized pistols only) are taken up. Plates of food are dropped or often ditched. (The latter are carelessly abandoned for an adult to come across and gather up.) Most of the youngest have sticky-turned-filthy hands from overly sweetened, inevitably spilled punch.

Eventually the darting about winds down when it's time for the ceremony: fifth grade graduation. The twelve or so "seniors" form a line in alphabetical order and a makeshift stage has been placed before the audience of parents, siblings, and any younger students who are calm enough to sit still (this last category does not include many).

The occasion is jubilant, without doubt. But as concerns the adults, blended into the overall mood is more than a trace of nostalgia. All of us, it seems each parent without exception, thinks backward to the five-year-olds that only minutes before sprinted from infancy, raced past toddlerhood only to begin school. More than a handful wipe away tears. Our kids are now ten. And…there is no way of keeping them ten or, better yet, turning back time.

The class will disperse, but only the adults truly understand this. The kids will spread out, enter into a number of schools. Friendships will die away. New attachments will form.

But also, a much-loved innocence predetermined to die away looms ominously. Unavoidably. Permanently. And altogether too impatiently. In truth, it is already that for most of the girls, this leaving childhood behind has gained hasty momentum.

How did this girl "sophistication" sneak up? It is now that the *no-longer-a-mere-fifth-grader* girl pack sets itself apart. And clustered tightly into their private, no outsiders allowed clutch, they inevitably discuss matters of importance: shades of eye shadow, the merits of various mascaras. Do you apply cream or powder blush? Cell phones are crucial, namely "who are your favorites?" Clothes are judged, always clothes, and yes, music. Inevitably younger girls or girls who reject the pack (or vice versa) are targets of more than a fleeting, collective eye roll and shared around is the fact that mothers are deserving of this too. Mothers, I will add, who just provided nourishment...

True to form, the ten-year-old boys each seize a rubber playground ball which they then lob (say hurl) at one another. Preferably this is pitched from close range...at the head. If possible it reaches the eyes and, with any luck, will leave a glowing red patch. They aim food and they fling punch and then follow up with the plate and the cup... (Go ahead, leave it where it lands!) Music is worthy of discussion. Video games (violent) have meaning. This though, is weighed only when they tire of annihilating one another.

As concerns Grant, my oldest, multifaceted, profoundly sensitive child, he does not join the boys. Thrashing his friends? Positioning himself to be thrashed? He has not a bit of interest. Mixing with the girls then? This option? He turns lifeless.

He has, instead, isolated himself. And it is soon enough when I spot him just so. Utterly alone. As I move close he looks up and I see tears. With evident agony he asks me to explain the reason people have to grow up. I offer no response as we both know his question is entirely rhetorical. He helps me pack away our serving dishes, our plates, and then, what has now become customary, we are the first to leave.

As we drive home I think over the painful reality that within three fleeting, impatient months, middle school will begin. It will be then that these very kids, these young, young children will begin to eat each other alive. (Consider *Lord of the Flies*.) Some will survive this better than others but not one will remain unscarred as they start to understand what the adults can't bear to reveal: Life gets hard, very. People are complicated, too often mystifying, even adults. From time to time the world itself will be impossible to understand. And there will be times the world will be at once purposefully and purposelessly cruel. And now they will need to navigate this, and at times, they will need to do so alone.

Unbearably I recognize that in this time, short and passing, it is assured that my child above all, my young, compassionate, gentle child, will be one the wolves devour whole. And these predators will lie in wait, and they will attack greedily, and they will do so without a moment's delay.

fifteen

Middle School

And so it arrives: the irrational, unavoidable mess of the sixth, seventh, and eighth grades. And, as known, our children are all of eleven years-old when this chaos comes crashing down. As for Grant in particular, this age is much too young. Distressingly he is much too vulnerable. How can one resolve the conundrum of a child who is academically years beyond his peers but all the while socially years behind? Dispiritingly I will find no one ever who is able to offer a solution.

But despite this known disparity, there is undeniably much weightier anguish in him than this alone can account for, and this is realized as he begins to lose his equilibrium. Grant's balance, it seems, is affected by whatever is off balance inside, whatever entity unknown that has taken over the whole of him. It's as if each and every cell within his mind, his heart and soul will be, from this day forward, regulated by an unexplained unsteadiness. He falls off chairs. He trips. At times his speech too circles and spins, as if his thoughts somersault in advance of all else. As time moves forward this will lessen; later still it will stop altogether.

Looking back I believe this had to do with panic, an all-encompassing terror, owing to the inexplicable incongruency between his body and his brain. Every bit of this, while knowing, despite all anguish, regardless of any pleading, he must—no way going around it—he will grow older.

I find a physical therapist who sees too that he struggles to find balance. This happens in particular, she determines, when his eyes are closed. She establishes that, at these times, his body "floats," and it's true, according to him, during such occasions he does, in fact, feel a disconnect from Earth. (*It's as if he lives a world apart.*)

So somehow his body, newly separated from his mind, has forgotten how to exist within its surroundings. The physical therapist works with him. Eventually Grant will take yoga. Balance is a challenge. The flow is difficult. But he makes progress. The classes are small and strictly limited to others his age. The environment is safe, emotionally. He looks forward to the hour he spends there.

As time progresses he will participate in Tae Kwon Do; upward movement is achieved here too. He progresses two belt levels. He joins lap swimming at a pool relatively close to his school. I drive him to one of these activities every afternoon and, all the while, Parker is dragged along. Eventually Parker will join Grant in Tae Kwon Do and swimming but I know this is not enough. (The injustice is, in every way, a gnawing presence, gritty and improper. And yes, it does evolve that this inequality becomes a family standard, so that this wrongful and injurious arrangement will persist to further wound us all.)

When one is broken, all are broken. Each of us has come to understand this at our very foundation.

sixteen

Downward

Throughout middle school Grant is able to circumvent his pain for days in succession, but too he strives for his place among others. He endeavors to participate in life. Some activities that have habitually interested him continue to do so. Intermittently. Many he avoids, has lost interest in altogether. In order to cope, he works to hide from himself, from others, his suffering. More and more he overshadows his pain with his intellect. But there are flare-ups. Outward confusion, anger, and tears will inevitably surface and overwhelm. He smiles. He cries. He is unsettled. Fearful. Disruptive. Hyper-active and then lethargic. (*When one then always the opposing other.*) In every possible way he baffles me.

In every possible sense he devours me.

There are the handful of students who entered into this same school. The boys, the girls, those who were once his friends in younger grades, they begin to avoid him. Every one. He is flustered, nervous. Sensitive. A weak link. A target. Someone not to be "seen with" unless you wish to be branded the same. He is bullied. He is laughed at. He is complex. He is delicate and he is boisterous, one and next the other.

And so isolation surges, self-imposed and yes, otherwise. He has a "friend" (who shuns him). The father of this boy does not know the social turn of events that have befallen Grant since the gentler years of grade school. This father's son struggles in science and so he makes a suggestion to the instructor: Possibly his son and Grant can work together? The teacher explains that Grant gets "it" before he himself, but no one understands how his brain works in order for him to arrive at his conclusions. From this teacher's observation it would be impossible for Grant to explain his methods, which seem intuitive, spontaneous. Instantaneous. So it comes to haunt, over again, that his intellect, these intuitive, spontaneous, instantaneous qualities further isolate him, further prevent him from engaging with peers.

Nevertheless, there are two friends who will stick by his side for a lifetime. The first of the two is a boy from elementary school. A friend who, while there, had stuttered. Grant had protected this boy from the all-too-inevitable ridicule he had endured. This boy does not attend the same middle school as Grant. His high school will be a different one. Nonetheless their friendship will remain intact. In truth, over the years, all starting in elementary school, this boy's family has been Grant's second "people." His second protectors. Their house, his second home.

But all this acceptance… This doesn't exist at school.

Here, he is on his own.

And that is the reason I have meetings, many meetings with both teachers and administrators. Grant is asked to select a teacher to become his confidant and his ally. Instantly he makes his choice: a woman, his history instructor.

She adores my son, this teacher. She tells me "he is honest to a fault." He had made a correction to a grade she had marked for him on a test. She had given him more points than he had a right to. (He cannot be tricked with numbers!) He is kind and he is polite, he is silly and he is sad…not qualities describing those who are "most popular" in middle school. But he is smart. Enjoyable for an *adult* to converse with.

This teacher is there for him whenever he feels the need to talk. Which he does. And which he does do, periodically. But being seen with adults too often doesn't help elevate status. Mostly he is alone.

Mostly…he is the farthest-reaching ball.

seventeen

Only He Knows

T*his*" is something difficult, say impossible, to imagine. "*This*" is a thing the widespread population will never experience. Never comprehend. Never feel the weight of, nor the acute and overwhelming suffering attached to it. And this "suffering," this is inescapable from the "*thing*" itself, an every-single-moment of every-single-day of every-single-year, kind of suffering. And too, this "suffering," this is suffering from which the sufferer will never be free.

Ever.

And this is his one and his only life, Grant, my son, the one who suffers.

Living as transgender in and of itself is not the only lonely, unbearable aspect for an individual. Not by an impossibly long margin.

Hand in hand is ridicule. Stigma. Shame. Low self-esteem. Self-hatred. Stunted emotional growth. Stunted social growth. Fear of attachment. Fear of loneliness. Failure at school. Acute anxiety. Profound depression. Intense anger, primarily directed at the mother (me). A deep and limitless neediness (again, me). Social anxiety. Phobias, sometimes of *everything*. Rational fear, unquestionably. Sometimes anorexia. At times weight gain.

Others will claim this is a "choice": Man-up!

There is verbal abuse. Emotional abuse. Physical abuse. "Failure to launch." Thoughts of suicide. Attempts of suicide. And suicide, unfathomable numbers of suicide.

And Grant is now entering puberty when all this gender complexity matters heavily.

He begins to avoid girls now, at once wanting to be included among them, but all the while knowing he can't. As for his classmates? More and more they are engaging with the opposite sex, kids are "coupling up, going steady" while Grant continues to remain on hold.

And I have no idea he is terrified. Terrified of what is happening both inside him and taking place around him. His inability to participate in it. His otherness. More and more he hides in his room, insulates himself there. As always he is with his computer, continuously silent. And next my standing in his doorway staring down at his motionless body. My questions. My pleading.

It comes about then, owing to his anguish, his fear, his isolation, all owing to his *gender dysphoria*, that this is the time he shuts himself down utterly, and in doing just that, he will remain "twelve" for years to come.

Until age twenty-four, the year (s)he decides to confront all.

Discouragingly, it will be only then, still twelve years ahead, when I will realize what Grant had been experiencing during those years, his struggles, his terrors. The cause of his misery. The reason that, despite my attempts to pull him back into the world, he wasn't able to reemerge. But for now, confusion pervades me as much as failure defines me. I am not only at a loss, I *am* lost.

As puberty advances, he works ever-more diligently to stifle his pain. This is self-preservation. This is fighting to survive. He knows he is "out of the ordinary" at an age when nothing other than ordinary is tolerable. He is plagued by the thought he will be singled out as the "outcast." The "freak."

He is tormented by the fear of rejection.

But rejection is inevitable.

And this particular rejection? This is not something attached solely to the stormy years of puberty. No, the dire importance of conformity, it seems, is not generation-specific.

And often, way too often, this rejection is not limited to outside the family.

This, the grand majority of all this, is what confronts my son/daughter as (s)he reaches the already impossible years of the sixth, seventh, and eighth grades.

But she does survive them.

Barely.

I too live through them.

But only just.

eighteen

Trial and Error
and Error...

There is a unit of study during the second year of middle school that focuses on the Middle East. The sixty or so seventh graders spend time researching several aspects of the region. At the end of the three-week period parents are invited to visit booths set up by the kids. Each station provides unique insight into the area. When the amount of time allotted to peruse booths ends, students and parents sit down to a meal: food emblematic to the region of study.

The kids, now at an age where the presence of parents both humiliates and taunts them, inevitably cluster together in one section of the auditorium. The adults, parents and teachers alike, then gather in another.

But, it is as soon as Grant has filled his plate, that he moves in my direction, bypassing his classmates. Confusingly, and not just a bit self-consciously, I make space beside myself. He stays with me throughout the meal. My reassurance, the safe haven I provide, my acceptance—all this desperately outweighs any interaction with peers.

His deepest wish then is to avoid others altogether, to avoid school. Sidestep his life. He falls ill a lot. At least this is what he claims. Teachers and extended faculty ask me why he's missed so many days. Our family doctor instructs me to send him unless his temperature is higher than 101 degrees. Which I do. Which I do despite the inevitable morning battles we undergo…the never-to-engage-in power struggles I consistently face, those power struggle "games" that every "almighty parenting expert" and each "appreciative of my world" psychologist has sternly counselled against. (*Go ahead, judge me*! …*Get a grip, Sandra*…)

He becomes a know-it-all. He lives inside his head in order to circumvent his inner suffering. Understandably this "knowing-it-all" is off-putting to the other kids, who would like to be acknowledged for knowing a few things as well, which of course they do. His father and I highlight his intellect too, both to him and to ourselves. This helps us cope as well. (*At least he's smart*, we tell ourselves, we say to one other. *At least he is very smart*.)

As time progresses, his want of separation only intensifies. This is living "*a world apart.*" This is his "*private world of agony.*" An agony where others do not exist, a pain where others don't matter; a wall formed of intellect and unrelatability. Of fear.

There is a day his science instructor gives a lecture. Grant has a question which is independent from the discourse. Grant leaves his seat and walks to the front of the classroom. He asks his teacher "in private" his question. The teacher is then forced to stop lecturing in order to tell Grant this must wait until later.

"This leaving your seat, this interrupting, is not helpful to either of us," he explains. My psychologist tells me this is classic anxiety in action. Another insists it is Attention Deficit Disorder. Indisputably.

What do I believe? Why does it need a label? *Just fix it!*
At least he is smart...

I find a doctor, a child psychologist, who works with kids on a scale of problems such as anger management, social difficulties, ADD, ADHD, mood disorders, and anxiety disorder, to list a handful. This doctor's diagnosis? Grant indeed has ADD as well as anxiety disorder. So they converse, this doctor and Grant, but mostly Grant spends the one hour, twice a week, engaged in a process known as *neurofeedback.*

As for Parker? He is again, all over again and unceasingly again, dragged along. And too, as if he knows he shouldn't complain (Mom is weary, Mom is handling all that she is able), he never does.

During these sessions Grant sits in front of a computer. There is a game in front of him which he is asked to play. Not surprisingly he is enthusiastic toward this and so looks forward to his time there. Placed on his head are sensors, four total. The readings from these sensors are fed onto a screen that the doctor then monitors. What appears on this screen is Grant's brain activity. The purpose of this procedure is to teach how to self-regulate behavior. When these sensors read his brain activity as too "revved-up," too "stimulated," the doctor will alter the course of the game, lessen its "hype" in order to help quiet the mind. The ultimate objective is to help the child recognize the point at which his mind soars so that he can bring it back to a calmer state. Then, over time, with all this in-session practice, ideally the child will have the ability to deescalate his mind away from any unwanted hyper activity, or anxiety-based tumult that is certain to confront him outside the office, and to do so drug free.

Ideally.

So in theory this is a perfect solution for a parent who would like to avoid putting drugs in their child's young, still-much-to-develop, brain.

In theory.

But *my* child? *My* child is unlike others. Continuously inimitable. His stress, his anxiety, his inability to sit still and concentrate…this is directly related to the fact that this is puberty and he is living in the wrong body, and he doesn't yet understand what all this means. And he is terrified.

The sessions end. Our discouragement lingers.

But what will be yet more discouraging later, at this point eleven years ahead, the time Grant will reveal all, is that he had expressed to this doctor during the time of their sessions that he felt he was female, and that he had felt this way since the time he was old enough to understand there was a difference to be had. Three, maybe four years of age.

As for me? I have been told that my son has Attention Deficit Disorder and Anxiety Disorder. Period. And yes, these concerns existed as well. He did struggle with both. Every bit outwardly and visibly so. And I was, will be, for the many years that will still elapse yet after puberty, single-mindedly determined to find a drug-free solution to these problems. That which I am without any knowledge is that my searching, every single one of my efforts, will be forever futile, whether drug-free or otherwise. A solution, I will one day learn, is unattainable. The underlined reality, the *actual issue*, is both unchangeable and one that I have not been informed exists.

But I will try. Exhaustively, exhaustingly, I will try.

So I next haul Grant (Parker) to acupuncture sessions. These sessions begin with a few quick minutes of *muscle testing*, an exercise that will expectantly pinpoint to the practitioner the area of the body where "toxins" exist and, as follows, where the needles will be targeted. When placed exactly, pathways will open within the body and, by doing so, release the contaminants which are at the root of his troubles.

Out of sheer desperation I choose to believe this will help.

Months pass.

Chiropractic appointments follow. But this is a sort of chiropractic application that focuses on *nerve interference*. When applied, I am informed, this specialized type of chiropractic treatment works to heal a larger spectrum of ailments than the traditional approach. In this case the spine is manipulated in order to connect with nerves that interfere with health: physical as well as mental, as well as emotional. The credence is that these "interfered with" nerves have been "frozen" in time, rigid, due to past injuries (physical or emotional). When cleared of deep-rooted, repressed memory, these nerves can then begin anew in a healthy manner. In other words, no more ADD or Anxiety Disorder based on emotional nerve injury.

Again. Nothing.

And I am losing ground. Ever increasingly I am terrified I will never find a solution. And too, added to all is Grant's silence. His *unremitting silence*. His motionlessness. Silence due to fear. Silence over a sense of powerlessness. Silence and motionless over his inability to truly comprehend what is at the root of all that is wrong, a detachment from himself? A *gender incompatibility*?

I deeply fear he will never be happy and, by extension, neither will I. Moreover, it is excessively that I am alone in this battle. Robert works hard. He flies from city to city, from state to state, always engaged in work. Endlessly buried in work. Parker's existence is blurry as he remains out of focus. Out of *my* focus. And I am broken. We are broken. And I am losing strength.

Sluggishly I continue my search for relief.

But, since it seems I cannot, or refuse to, learn from prior "cures," those all-too-dispiriting remedy attempts, I proceed to drag him to yet another "healer."

And this is when he undertakes hypnosis. (*This will be it*, I tell myself. *Finally I have landed on the perfect fix.*)

Months go by. Time is consumed. Money is spent…

Then begins the never-desired and endless series of medications that Grant will try out, abandon, try out…abandon…try out and abandon.

The three or so ADD medications he takes, staying with each for weeks at a time, come to prove either non-effective or produce in him a sense of disconnectedness. A disconnect between his mind and his body. A disconnect between mind and body that already exists by way of being transgender. And then too, this "disconnect," it works to further increase the adverse "floating" sensation against which he already battles.

Anxiety Disorder is targeted. Medications are ingested, one and next another, all in advance of finding partial, transitory improvement.

Eventually, as prescribed, he tries depression medications. Again there is trial and there is error before some degree of relief comes about. (This following a gradual and undesirable upping of dosages, this following the many, way too many appointments that, over the years, will continue on and on and confusingly on, with invariable and minimal improvement.)

Because the actual issue lies elsewhere.

As Good as Ritual

Robert attempts to comfort me. He does this, yes, as among the two of us it is my own pain that is most visible. He strives to calm me because he sees my anguish. Because this anguish, by now, this surfaces exceedingly often. In truth, it has become as good as ritual. Exhausting, ominous routine.

He's good with hugs, Robert. His voice sooths as he reassures over and over that Grant will be fine. "He is smart, very smart. There will be a point he will soar." But Robert, he hasn't repeatedly witnessed the day to day despair that Grant suffers. He has not routinely experienced the day to day ruin of Grant's non-life. I lie on our bed and I cry. Mascara runs down my face, stains the spread, the sheets.

This is seventh grade. The year Grant has no friends. The year I have multiple, believe endless, meetings with faculty. The year Grant has selected his history teacher (a woman) as his confidant. And this is the evening following the afternoon lunch where he had bypassed his classmates in order to sit beside me.

"Trust that everything will turn out okay." Robert says this.

But I don't trust...I don't believe "everything will turn out okay" because it is by now that I have seen too much of the other.

nineteen

Encouragement Before Discouragement

During a subsequent trip to the mountains we run into a family we know from home. A family that has a daughter the same age as Grant, and she has brought along a friend. There comes a time during the chilly afternoon we ski when the daughter decides to head to the base of the hill, the lodge there, in order to warm herself. Her companion, however, is not ready to quit for the day. It is decided then that she should ski awhile longer. Grant, who, as known, routinely avoids peers, offers to ski with her. We are astonished by this, understandably so. And then visibly the two have a great time in each other's company. I am elated!

That evening, however, the opposite occurs. Every time it seems we must eddy around. How did I miss the inevitable?

The "opposite" occurs during dinner. We have decided to gather with this family at the home where we stay. Close to the main table we have set up a smaller table where the two girls and my two sons will eat. But it is as soon as our guests arrive that Grant says he's lost his appetite. Quietly he then retreats to another room in the house where he remains until our friends, the girls in particular, have left.

And next his silence…

Our encouragement, turned our discouragement, turned his silence… This now circles back unendingly. (*So why am I continuously caught off guard? Astonished?*) How is it that, uncompromisingly, I am thrown deeper and deeper into the haze that overwhelms and clouds my mind? *When will I see?*

But I don't see, and I don't see because I don't know where to look. And I reject defeat. I *will* this of myself, *I demand this of myself.*

Therefore, when Grant is in eighth grade, and as we encounter another reason that inspires, I again grasp to the intangible.

The two French teachers, I learn through Grant, will take students the upcoming summer to France, any student who wants to go is welcome. The trip will last three weeks, one of which will be spent with a host family. Grant is enthusiastic, passionate! He wants to go!

And…he has a good time!

He is on ADD medicine when this occurs, one that he sticks with until it no longer proves effective. But this is before that time, the time before it no longer proves effective. So he is calm and he is focused and likely aided by this, he makes a friend, a boy who has only joined the school that same year. The group takes several days to get acquainted with Paris and for many hours each day the students pair off to do so. He and his new friend are ready to go, set to explore the city unsupervised and I am all in. In with the independence, the companionship, the *friendship.* His *enthusiasm.* I am reminded then of the years he was interested in all things. *Everything!* There is an afternoon he calls from Paris, I can hear every bit of this in his voice.

While with the host family, he swims with the two brothers in their community pool. He is introduced to their friends. The family takes him on a trip to the Mediterranean. He plays chess with the father. They talk politics (and agree).

Then, it is three years following this trip when we receive a phone call. This is his host family on the line. They would like Grant to revisit.

Three years later, however, Grant is in a bad way. His depression, his anxiety…these are incapacitating.

He declines.

And throughout the years moving forward, his symptoms will worsen still. His depression, his anxiety, these will comingle heartlessly with the phobias that will overpower only to isolate him entirely. Because these phobias, they will extend everywhere, they will encompass everything and they will come to be of everyone.

This is our future…

But for now, as I am blind to this future, since I cannot envision the added suffering it will carry with it, I continue allowing myself times to soar. And I do so determinedly. I do so urgently, and I do so *stubbornly*. Therefore when my two-pound, nine-and-a-half-ounce preemie has risen to a height of six feet two, is introduced to crew, and decides to go ahead, I do just that.

In addition to his grand height, he is lean and he is muscular, the body of an athlete and a perfect candidate to row. "He will get outside, he will socialize." Robert and I are overjoyed! I find a carpool to divide up the chauffeuring, but still, there remain two to three afternoons each weekday when I drive him (Parker) to the lake.

He is sixteen now and, as in prior years, he maintains his flow between his sensitive feminine interior and his decidedly masculine exterior. All jumbled together, of course, is his unsettled identity, an identity which he is certain no person, historical or present, has ever felt. An identity confusion he continues to guard tacitly.

Later, long after my years of nagging, my beseeching, our heated anger, our pain and our tears, all during which I will have asked, "What is wrong?" (s)he will talk to me about her confusion, a confusion that will have persisted much further into the future than I would have understood. It is only then when I will truly comprehend "his" silence, "his" fear of exposing himself, his terror over the prospect of rejection.

But, for now, the extent of which I understand is that he suffers and the extent of which he understands, is that there is something innately within him that is not present in others. And he is frightened.

Although withstanding his confusion, his pain and anxiety… his "*otherness*," there are times he presses himself to play exclusively the masculine role. His aspiration is to be "normal," to *feel* "normal"; for others to see him *as* "normal." A normality that should be true for him, as is true for "all others."

While embodying his masculine side he often "overcompensates," ramps up his masculinity a stretch further than is common in most boys. This, as a way to make up for his heartfelt shortcomings. So he appears "all in," wills himself to be just that. His voice has deepened now, a man's voice, and he embraces this change toward his outward goal. He is boisterous, rowdy. He cheers others on. He high-fives. He rows hard.

At first.

This is what he does. At first. Up until the time his/her true identity screams to be acknowledged, if only to herself. She awakens then to her surroundings. She awakens to the disconnect that exists between herself and these determined male athletes, these fearless guys who exhibit rough and often crude camaraderie. And this overwhelms.

There comes an afternoon when the coach calls. This occurs an hour or so after practice has begun. "Has Grant come by the house?" He hasn't. But neither, I am told, is he any longer at the boat house. Grant hadn't returned along with the team once they had set out on a six-mile run. My son is MIA.

I head to the lake. By the time I arrive he is with the coach, having turned up an hour and a half after the others, the entirety of them.

But he is there.

He had run his six miles, like the rest, but he had taken them leisurely. Separated himself out from the others.

He had a lot to think over…

When out of earshot I ask the coach if my son has been a victim of ridicule, "picked on" by the other boys. He responds, "I've seen worse. In truth, he is well liked. He's a nice kid. But too, he is difficult for the others to understand."

Grant finishes the fall season.

He doesn't return in spring.

And I remain oppressed by my lack of knowledge, my powerlessness to help and, as always, by his silence.

His silence.

There are times his silence pushes me to a place of irretrievable anger. Anger at him. Anger at the world. Anger at *our* world. And one of these head-butting, anger-provoking impasses is centered around a driver's license or, more accurately, the lack thereof. And, owing to *his* anger, his *absolute stubbornness* and his *insufferable silence* over this, I believe, wholeheartedly, his refusal to drive is singularly and utterly due to a disrespect of me and of my time.

Yet, I am conflicted, because *I am frantic for him to get out.* And therefore I drive him. *Frustratingly, begrudgingly, I drive him.* Because yes, I need him out of the house. Out of his room. Off his computer. I need for him to *do something…*

Therefore when there is a day he wishes to visit the University of Washington, I, as would be foreseeable, *drive him…*

Not unexpectedly he plans to study both mathematics and science while in college. But despite my/his father's insisting, he refuses to concede that grades are a large part of the acceptance criteria. He doesn't think all that will matter much. "I know everything I will need to know." (*Oh come on!*) So apparently this brilliance of his has gaps. Deep, profound chasms.

During his visit, he is allowed access into the chemistry building, the labs there, in the company of a guide. The various science and mathematics departments are, of course, eager to attract enthusiastic, bright minds into their programs.

He observes a room where PhD students are looking at giant screens and various monitors; they are tapping on keyboards, all with the aim of discovering new cancer treatments via the use of nanotechnology. As his tour nears its end, he asks the guide if he can linger, observe a while longer, and permission is granted.

He remains another hour while the PhD students involve him in conversation, answer his questions. Take in his enthusiasm.

As he exits the building I can see his elation. His eyes express this. His posture says this too. He is eager to talk. He tells me "this is *exactly* what I want to do." He is high for the following two days, maybe more.

At home our neighbor, a doctor, asks Grant, "Would you like to intern this coming summer at the hospital?" This occurs a few days following his visit to the university; this is after I have described to this woman his enthusiasm while there.

When she leaves us I ask Grant, "Would you like to do that?" His face creases with the agony he feels. His brows lower, as does his head. "Yes, I want to so much, but I can't Mom, I just can't."

What is wrong with my son?

twenty

Two Fleeting Years

There are two years, two magnificent but fleeting years when I am lucky to spend time with Parker exclusively. Those are the years we have six hours each weekday. Just the two of us. The years before Grant turns eight, the time before I will feel Grant's misery as if it is my own and his neediness as if it's an insatiable black hole, the strength of which will untiringly draw me further and further toward its center. The years prior to my terrors over the possibility of suicide and my undivided hyper-attention with Grant in order to assure he will remain alive. Two innocent years before I will begin to sense the power of the deluge to come... Those are *our* two years, Parker's and mine.

We drop Grant at school, his first and second grades, and this is the moment our six hours begin. We go to the playground, maybe the Museum of Science. It could be that together we visit friends who have children Parker's age. Even grocery shopping is a fun adventure with Parker. "Sneakily" (with audible laughter) he picks out items within reach to toss in the cart. (The majority of which, when looking away, I return to their shelves and are then quickly forgotten.)

There is a day when Parker is four. He wears the Halloween

costume he had only just adorned the week before to amass candy. We pull away from school, he in his costume smiling and proud.

Soon we're in a line outside the Children's wing of the Museum of Science where eagerly we wait to enter.

But while standing there it is almost immediate when Parker turns to me with tears streaming his face. I bend down then, level with him. "That person said I'm cute." He points to his left... *Well of course he is cute! He is a four-year-old zebra for the sake of...*and so I am baffled over the tears. A zebra. The costume he had enthusiastically chosen. The black stripes that I meticulously painted onto the white backdrop of a "onesie." The hat and tail we miraculously found.

He is adorable!

"I don't want to be cute, I want to be scary!"

I fight back my amusement because his disappointment is so real, so overwhelming. "Next year you can be a bear, maybe a tiger?" I say to him, "Either, I assure him, will most certainly be scary."

The following year he transforms into a T-Rex. *Perfect...* We avoid places where a misguided someone may mistake him for cute. All goes smoothly.

We read dinosaur books, countless dinosaur books. I pull him close, put my free arm around him, and we read. And we do so over and over until Parker has all the stories memorized. Until he can pronounce each multi-syllable dinosaur's name better than I can.

And, of course, there is his fascination, *his passion*, with construction. And, as such, when we come across a construction in progress (not infrequently) Parker, from his car seat, points out the work site. At times I park somewhere close by where we stand for a while outside the barrier fence. I lift him up so that he can see the excavators below in the hole, the dump trucks that wait, one at a time, to receive the unwanted dirt. Often we spot cement trucks preparing for their turn at the action. The backs rotating, mixing the heavy gray mass. We watch on as workers wearing yellow hard hats move about, carting various equipment. I revel in Parker's enormous smile.

We buy construction books and weave them into our dinosaur time.

There are additional occasions, those other than our cherished six hours. There is the long weekend Parker and I alone go to the San Juan Islands.

The islands—San Juan, Orcas, Lopez, and Shaw—are a two hours' drive north and a ferry ride away from Seattle. While there we create sculptures in the sand. Search for shells and agates. We discover starfish and sea anemones and we watch seals at play. We swim—but we do not swim in the frigid waters of Puget Sound, rather in the warmth of the pool at the inn where we stay. For dinner Parker and I share crab or a basket of fish n' chips prepared from that day's catch in Fisherman's Bay on Lopez Island.

That was a magnificent weekend with Parker.

Those were magnificent years with Parker.

Those years were fleeting...

twenty-one

Just Do It!
(For the Love of...)

Yes, I want Grant to drive! Get *himself* places! I want this *immensely*! I need to be free of this ceaseless chauffeuring, this dragging along of Parker. This *constant need of me*. But still he refuses to get his license. He *refuses*. And he is adamant. Despite having taken driver's education the year prior, despite that he *can* drive, he refuses. Flat out.

And therefore it won't happen. And it will continue to not happen. Until (s)he is twenty-seven years old.

By now he has three friends and the times he goes out (not often) they offer to drive. He takes the city bus to school…when he shows. He rides the bus to his psychologist…on the days he decides to surface. But ever increasingly are the times he tells me he won't go to school, to his appointments. He refuses to get to the bus, to ride the bus. And again *his silence* followed by my probing, my nagging, my anger, which does nothing but incite *his* anger. He is humiliated by his fears. I will learn later about his terror of strangers, of the outside world. However, since I continue to read his reticence, his refusal, his obstinacy, as a simple and blatant callousness toward me *I don't want to drive him.*

Anywhere! And still, the result of all his reluctance, his heightened emotion, just as in earlier years, is to keep my attention solely with him. I want to walk away from this, from him! But I can't. He needs to get to school, to his doctors.

And therefore I live with panic. I cannot bear for him to miss. So *I drive him.* To school, to his psychologist, his psychiatrist. Unendingly I worry over his mental health, his emotional well-being. *So I drive him.* As for school, this is five times each week times two. As for appointments, there are two a week. I am incensed over this. I am exhausted, fearful, and incensed. All at once.

There comes a day he tells me he will get downtown on his own. This happens, of course, following weeks and weeks of his refusal and weeks and weeks of my subsequent impatience. And this happens mostly to avoid my harassment.

But it is soon enough when I discover that he doesn't get himself downtown, he doesn't get to his doctor's office and he doesn't do this because he feels he cannot. Instead he contacts his doctor by phone. I am not aware this has occurred, this appointment by phone. In fact, I believe he's made it downtown because he's left the house. But what I learn later is that he's gone as distant as the far end of the yard and hides from me there behind and under a tree. And too, it is also later when I learn that a session held by phone is not covered by insurance. When I confront him about the extra charge he admits what he's done. He agrees not to do it again. He does it again. More than once. He wants, he *needs* to talk with his doctor. He tells me this.

Eventually it is my own psychiatrist who tells me I need to stop all this running him everywhere, this making sure he attends school, his sessions. So mostly I do. But again, I worry and I worry, and then occasionally I break the agreement. And the times I don't break the agreement? The times he stays home? Those are the times I become physically ill.

I have a friend whose son will not move an inch to get his driver's license; he refuses to bother. My son and hers are now high school seniors, eighteen years old. So my friend, she lets all this "refusal" go until it becomes too much of a bother for her. And this is when she lays down the law. Her son then, he goes to the DMV the following week and drives off.

She instructs me to *lay down the law* with Grant. But she, as no one to date, has any idea what I'm up against.

By twenty-one we are willing to buy him a car. But no. Still there is no reward, no bribe, neither punishment nor consequence that will push him forward. But too, by the time he has reached twenty-one, I have not one notion that his phobias have elevated to a level so as to paralyze him entirely.

And as I have no clarification my anger only intensifies and my impatience simply mounts with each sluggish day.

And I am tired. I'm tired of worrying and I'm tired of nagging because I have been doing both for too long.

There is Grant's high school sophomore year, for instance. The year the students are divided into two separate tracks for English. The time when I learn Grant, *naturally*, is not among those who are headed into the advanced program.

I pester him.

Yet again.

And I do so over the sheer inexplicability of it, and I do so over his unrelenting lack of caring. And, *as always*, by his silence...

Next I speak with the instructor. And this is when I confirm what I had already known. "Grant should be on the list for my course," she says. "In fact, he should be so above any other tenth grader." She explains that his comments on the literature examined, the conclusions at which he arrives, are elevated well beyond all other students. "He thinks in abstraction," she adds. "He is able to do this despite that this way of thinking is years ahead of his age. "Abstract thinking," she lets known, "typically occurs much later. And then too, it's not altogether uncommon to encounter those who are never able to achieve it. "His comments regularly challenge others to think, go deeper, move beyond the obvious."

"But," she says, then pauses. Before the sigh. "My students are required to write papers of criticism. This they are expected to do following the readings and the class discussion as regards the readings; at times they will be instructed to write up to ten pages."

She pauses again and I am altogether confused. "So what is the issue?"

"I have never been able to pull more than three sentences out of your son."

What!

Not three *pages*. Not three *paragraphs*. But three *sentences*? ("Why should I bother writing it all down Mom, I've already told the teacher what I think?")

Why bother? Well, let's see…perhaps so that you can be part of a class that might *challenge you a bit*? As opposed to one, for instance, that you are likely to *sleep through*? (*And still receive barely a passing grade.*)

He will not write (*in excess of three sentences*) because he doesn't want to.

And his unwillingness is exhausting. His lack of caring is infuriating. And I want nothing more than to disengage with every stubborn piece of him. But this can't happen, not now. Instead, right now I will walk down the hallway of his school to the biology classroom in order to revisit his need for remedial study.

His biology instructor has observed that Grant comes up short. (*For the love of...just do the work.*)

And so must I explain (to yet another teacher) that I am certain my son will not need a "booster shot" of biology. Despite his poor performance. Despite his grades. I attempt to make the argument.

This teacher then talks with Grant. They have a "biology conversation," the level of which surpasses Grant's age by many years. Remedial work is dismissed. But his grades? His participation? They continue to remain gloomy, dispirited. Like him.

And I cannot influence change.

And my parenting remains inadequate.

And I am tired.

twenty-two

He is Smart!
(At Least He is Very Smart...)

S eventh grade, this is advanced math.

The teacher has prepared a problem which he had pre-written across the expanse of two side-by-side chalkboards. It is twelve lines across, maybe more, one underneath the other. It has more symbols than it has numbers. The instructor's intention is to take the students through this equation step-by-step. The time allotted for this lesson is one week.

Grant enters the classroom. Studies the board. Within three minutes he takes chalk in hand and writes his answer. His answer is correct.

Graciously by tenth grade he is no longer ridiculed. But yet he sets himself apart, at once wishing and not wishing to mix with others. Still he is deeply anxious. This is both socially and academically. And the reason for academic anxiety? This, I eventually learn, is directly linked to his fear of leaving home, of leaving me: "As long as my grades stay low possibly I can live at home forever?"

For math he is placed in the twelfth-grade advanced track. The students, seventeen and eighteen-year-olds, having matured completely away from any middle school "don't let me be seen with the 'freak'" drama are accepting of him. In fact these kids, they respect Grant, admire his brilliance. He has humbled himself a bit; no longer does he need to know "everything." The upper-classmen and women assign him the title of genius. They ask for help with especially difficult problems. When they spot him in the hallway they say "Hi," ask "How's it going?" most often they follow up with "genius."

Bolstered by this acceptance his math grades improve...somewhat. And too, he becomes more comfortable with those who are older. This extends also to people who are younger. Both of these groups, as opposed to people his own age.

Although his social anxiety only mounts in college and while his grades remain as dismal as in high-school, during his sophomore year there he enrolls in an upper level English class. Just as before, there is in-class discussion concerning the readings before students will write their analysis, criticism of the work. Required for the first paper assigned are fifteen to eighteen pages. As customary with my son (although decidedly an improvement over high school) he comes up short, extremely short, as he hands the professor his *three pages* of writing.

Once read over, however, as soon as the professor has handed his paper back, this is when he learns he has been granted a 3.9. One small percentage point below the full 4.0. For *three pages* of writing. She will not award him the highest mark because his work is so very condensed. But despite all, and unexpectedly, she does give him next to the highest grade possible.

"How did you arrive at your conclusions regarding the reading?" She wants to understand this. The prof, she had not introduced the concepts, the inferences he had reached. The views of which he wrote, she imparted, were far advanced than she had intended to present below graduate school level. They were, in fact, akin to her own. His writing was concise, succinct, all that was needed to be said had been written down. Skillfully.

"It all seemed obvious" was his answer.

Okay...

Maybe he doesn't need to write in length?

Apparently, it seems, not this time around.

Seemingly, it appears, not with this prof.

Okay whatever...

He is smart!

At least he is very smart...

There is Respect

I have very little information about Grant's high school senior retreat, which remarkably he agrees to attend. But the most important detail is enough for me. In fact, it is everything.

There is a period during the two day excursion when the sixty or so seniors are asked to sit in a circle. Each student has been handed a piece of paper. On this paper is the name of a peer, a classmate. All have been instructed to write a message to that person, something positive. Something anonymous.

I learn of this "note writing" days later when I spot the folded paper on his dresser. He sits in his room while I pick it up and inquire about it. He tells me where it's from, the reason it exists. He says I can read it.

On his small paper reveals the compliment he was given. Be certain, this is an accolade any mother, anywhere, would wish for because it reads: *Grant is the type of person who does the right thing even when no one's looking.*

Yes, I cried.

twenty-three

Why is He so Very Afraid?

There is a unit of study that will culminate in an oral presentation. This is history class, ninth grade. There are maybe twenty students, no more, who make up this group. As the students finish their research, each, in turn, must stand before the others and present their findings. All are required to speak on average fifteen minutes.

The students will present in volunteer order. In other words, those who would like to get this "getting up in front of any peers" over with early on, can elect to do so. In contrast, those who would like to avoid the matter altogether, hoodwink themselves into believing their turn will never arrive, these will present toward the end.

And so I will merely say this…nearing the end of day five, each and every student has finished presenting, except the *very* last, which of course is, well, you know who…

Despite that silently Grant has willed away the inevitable, his inward pleading has come to no purpose. He is asked at once to stand in front of his classmates and begin.

He stalls. He begins to perspire. A few minutes pass and he remains seated. He is asked again, even encouraged to begin. Next with head down, eyes to the floor, he gives his presentation.

From his seat. It lasts two, maybe three, excruciating minutes.

Later by a few days, the instructor talks with me, "I don't know what demons haunt him. I wish I were able to help."

Neither of us understands the reason Grant wishes to disappear. And it will still be years before I will grasp what had been plaguing him for far too long by then…too many years before I will understand what he so desperately needed for me to realize even before puberty…he is beset for people to look at him only to not see him. This is his enduring hurt. This is his *insurmountable* hurt.

That same year (s)he scans the web in private. She searches for information: information that will explain how she feels, if at all obtainable. Her hope is to find others whose experience correspond to her own, in the case that others do exist. However, this is 2003, a time when not much knowledgeable information on the subject is offered. Still she does come to realize there is a name, transgender. She also learns that this way of being has existed always in the world.

She uncovers additional information as well, alarming information. And this is the time she comes to realize that in many parts of the world people are arrested for being so. Violence is often a fate they face. Murder by gangs or otherwise is not uncommon, whether inside prison or not. And this violence, this senseless, soulless murdering, this can happen anywhere. At home as well.

She manages to find a chat room where she proceeds to speak with people who are similar to herself, those who were born with physiques that do not match any sense of themselves. This gives her a certain comfort. She sticks with this group for years. Later she will meet up with some of these people face to face. Most are older, some become a type of mentor.

Despite the restrictive nature of this camaraderie, and although her newfound knowledge of violence, she yet braves to share her true identity with select others. She does this to "test the waters," and she does this with other "gamers" online. Computer gamers, all of which live in various locations across the globe. She chances approval. She fears rejection. And yes, she does receive both. But too, the rejection, the painful rebuffs she receives…these arrive in devastating, *terrifying* form, as some players refuse, flat out, to engage with her. Ever. And there is a boy from Germany who writes to "Grant" only to tell him that if he were to visit the US, he promises to hunt him down and then kill him.

Not without reason this is the time she descends ever deeper into her fears of the outside world, the greater population. How possibly can she admit who she is when confronted with the prospect of physical harm, possibly death? When *unquestionably* she will face additional rejection? Further emotional suffering and expanding condemnation?

Please God, hasn't my child suffered enough?

Haven't we all?

You Don't Always Get What You Need

Robert…again, and as always, yes, he comforts, he reassures, and all this attentiveness, this is good, welcomed. But too, this is not truly what I ask of him. This is not what I *have been asking* of him. This is not all that I need. And I tell him this. But he cannot hear me.

What I do need, that which I *desperately* need? This is Robert's staying around. This is his daily interaction with Grant. This is Robert's direct interaction with the school. It is his communicating directly with Grant's doctors.

I cannot do all this interacting, this communicating alone. This is incessant. This is breaking me. This renders any strength I may otherwise have nonexistent.

Robert flies here, he travels there. He works hard.

I am alone.

twenty-four

Some Time Ago

It has become difficult to remember our early years, Robert's and mine. The time we first met. The times we laughed, skied, traveled, went to movies and had dinners out. The handful of years as we married, had newborns, who quickly turned into toddlers, who then quickly turned school-aged. Mostly I can't imagine having known the joys of those days. Our extended years of trauma has all but erased them.

Will there be a day we retrieve them…those days?

Will either of us know the lightness we felt then?

Will there be a time we can leave Grant from under our collective watchful eye for even a minute?

How will we do this? This returning to the years when we felt a zest for life?

Were there, in fact, years before puberty hit our family too unbearably hard?

Will the heaviness subside?

Robert is truly my best friend. I admire in him immensely: his kindness, his brilliance—he earned an undue number of credits in college and, when all totaled, added up to three undergraduate degrees before his masters. Before his career launched. He was a mountain climber in those days.

Throughout our years of struggle, his passion for fly-fishing has never failed him, failed to be a necessary source of solace for him. Those fleeting but crucial hours of meditation that he so cherishes.

As for me? I have never found my solace. Not for a moment. For me there has only been heavy. My ever-lasting anxiety and fear. Nothing more than my own retreat from the world alongside Grant's.

I miss my earlier self. My earlier life.

Our earlier lives.

Our mutual enjoyments, Robert's and mine: of course, dinners out. Laughter. (*He thinks I'm funny, remember?*) We appreciate good wine. Neither of us would know how to live without a dog…ever!

Enjoyment…skiing, hiking, biking and travel. Being surrounded by friends. During those years…*some time ago*, it was not infrequently that we hosted parties…remember? But again, that was *some time ago*…up until our world turned on its head and we were no longer able to conjure a sense of fun. Before the lightness and sparkle vanished from Robert's eyes and his smile disappeared. Before mine did as well…

Will there ever be a day we will know lightness and sparkle?

That which I *do* know is, for now, we will continue through the heavy and the dark.

twenty-five

Six Months Away

And this is heavy, eleventh grade. This is dark. This is hard.

Hard to think about. Hard to write about.

Hard to have lived through. Barely we do.

He scarcely leaves his room that year. This starts in early winter and advances into spring. And beyond. During these months, which turn into years, he barely moves. He won't join us for dinner. He locks his door. He sleeps and he sleeps. And he sleeps. Marshaling energy to make a doctor's appointment is virtually impossible. He won't get up so that I can take him. He misses too often, way too often. He misses a lot of school. I worry he won't pass eleventh grade, whether he will graduate the following June. He doesn't graduate the following June. It will take him three additional months and a lot of hand-holding in order to do so.

All the while this persists, I retreat from my life as well. I don't go out. I do this out of fear he will hurt himself while I'm gone. And I do this because *a mother is only as happy as her unhappiest child.* And for these reasons I have no interest in my life, my friends. Myself.

And I am desperate for comfort. I turn then to my sister and to my mother. My need to talk is enormous and before long there is a day we spend an afternoon at my home. I bend forward as I sit. Through blurry eyes I look downward but I cannot see, or rather I do not register what's in front of me. My hands close together and press against my brow in order to shield my face. My body begins to rock front to back.

"Grant is worse, getting worse by the day. He will not talk, he will not leave his room. He does nothing, and every moment I fear he will take his life." Inevitably as I speak tears begin to streak my face, my breathing is restricted.

But I say all this, and I display my tears too, as if I cannot remember my mother will be fearful of my emotions, of the *strength* of my emotions. And then yes, it is immediate as her eyes well up, her face reddens as she reaches to cover her mouth. My sister embraces her reassuringly, protectively. They walk off, my sister shielding our mother from me, from my anguish. Her shoulders are curled inward, my mother's. I see her cry. I hear her cry. My sister surrounds her all the while. Hugs her.

There is nowhere safe.

I become overly sluggish. I need help. I do not and cannot find an answer to Grant's suffering. When I talk with my own psychiatrist I cry. All over I feel "if only I had done things right." My psychiatrist tells me I must "buck up," this for the reason, as he explains it, that as soon as I get better Grant will get better.

So it's confirmed. It *is* my fault. *All of it.* I believe this profoundly, thoroughly. Based on what my doctor has told me, I am now *certain* of this. I fall deeper into depression alongside Grant.

Why am I so very incompetent? Why can't I help my son? When, *how?* will I find the strength to buck up?

Will I ever do this mothering job right?

My anti-depressants too work for a while, until they don't. Until I must gradually wean myself from one before spending weeks building up to a level of effectiveness, or not, with another. My anxiety is also severe. I want to lie in bed all day long like Grant.

But I get up. I do things, not much. I must do more, I reproach myself. I must set an example for my son. And too, I am ashamed of my inactivity, I am tired of myself… Haven't I finally been enlightened as to the magical antidote? The surefire remedy? The cure all!? "As soon as I get better so will he." *So get up, Sandra!*

I talk with the school and explain what's going on. I attempt to speak with his psychologist, but I learn nothing. This because Grant is now an age where a doctor must have his permission to discuss with me anything; his doctor cannot tell me *a thing* because Grant refuses to give authorization.

But appear cheery, Sandra. *Fake it, damn it!* Fool yourself. Dupe the world. *Just do it! Only then will he get better.*

I begin to drink too much. My one or two glasses of wine turn into three or more…Robert does this too.

He escapes into work.

I am everything that is defeat.

And alone.

Even as he suffers ever-debilitating inertia, Grant continues to want higher education, he *needs* this and he tells us so over and over. But since neither his teachers, Robert, nor I have persuaded him (*implored* him) to look into one supplementary school other than our local university, indicates that his plan is to remain nearby.

Again there will be a time I will have information necessary to understand his wish to stay close. Only then will I appreciate that it is his prevailing hurt, his panic, raw and enormous, affixed to his/her gender complexity for which drifting too far from the safety of home, the security of father, of mother.

Of mother.

Would render any wandering off daunting, believe terrifying.

Moreover, since letting flee long-ago the notion of him attending a particular school for the genius in him, we are keenly on board with our local university, *would be* on board, rather, if this school were an option. Because this school is one of the best state universities in the nation, concerning many disciplines of study, math and science not excluded. It surpasses many private colleges as well. But what is also true is that a perspective student must have an average grade point of 3.7. Nothing less, often more, as well as impressive scores on the SAT in order to be yet looked at for acceptance. Grant's GPA? Not unexpectedly, this lies somewhere within the middle to lower 2s.

It is evening. The three of us, he, his father and I, we sit in the living room. The mood is somber. Again we come back to the subject of grades. "We told you so about the grades." Not what either of us actually says, but tempted, frustrated, furious? Oh yes. Yes, unquestionably yes. And that is one side of the two extremes we feel, as we vacillate between anger and unavoidable despondency. Inescapable fury and then compassion. We feel *all* this until we see how painfully he struggles with the application process. And this is when any anger, any thoughts of furious irony, any "we told you so" disintegrates, having been overpowered again by sorrow. Grant shrugs, looks away, stares downward. He is silent, impatient to leave the room. Avoid us, our questions. He will abandon our concerns, our disappointment, by walking away. He will use his computer as escape. He will numb himself through sleep.

I talk with the head of school; this occurs the following morning. "The filling in of an application should take an hour, maybe one and a half. Tops." We sit in his small office, his desk between us. Again my mood is downcast, visibly so. He too is serious. He too is concerned. "Grant has not completed a single application, although he began the process three months earlier," I tell him.

He checks Grant's grades; he winces. He checks his numbers on the SAT; once more I see, I hear, the wince. "This kid is one who could attend any school, anywhere, as long as acceptance were based solely on these scores."

We look at one another with confusion. I fight back tears. *What is wrong with Grant?*

Once home, I again put this question to him, like I've done so many times in the past. Once more I stand in his doorway as I speak. As customary, he lies on his bed. As usual his computer is propped before him. I move then and sit beside him. He doesn't look over. The keys on his computer click slowly, lifelessly, revealing his misery, the weight of which is unbearable. With brow furrowed, voice just audible, he says, "I don't *know* (why I sleep). I don't *know* (why I can't finish an application)." He doesn't know the reason he avoids his life; he doesn't know the reason he cannot spend time with others.

All this too said while evading my eyes, head lowered, staring vacantly at the screen before him. And this he does as if begging, *pleading*, as if beseeching me, to fix all.

But still, there remains his desire to get on with life, he tells us this. He wishes to engage with others, to finish an application, to be accepted into college. And how would he not want to attend college? This, when he's so good at thinking? At ideas? At reasoning and logic? Considering that a "too young to be wise" wisdom is merely part of who he is?

In the end he applies to two additional schools that are relatively close by. Schools where the acceptance criteria are not as rigorous. This he does as slowly and as painstakingly as he does with his desired, close-to-home university. It is as if he cannot bear to complete an application, but all the while he knows he must. And then he does. He finishes. At last.

But not wholly astonishing, even if greatly troubling, applications are completed and the send button pushed one short minute before deadline…11:59 PM, while Robert and I are sick with anxiety…

Although making the deadline, it is by late spring, four short months since all this application worry, when we are fraught to accept that any capacity to attend college the following fall will prove impossible. Grant is simply too sick.

Once more I'm summoned to a meeting at school. This is with the head of school as well as the school's psychologist. Grant rarely attends classes. Over and again he is found in parts of the school infrequently occupied. He has wound himself into a ball and is sound asleep. At times, he sleeps at his desk, waking only when the bell rings in order to make his way to the next class, or elsewhere in the building, to sleep. Again. The school psychologist attempts to talk with him but Grant is closed off. Sleepy. Unresponsive. He is all this despite his anti-depressant medications (plural). They are helpful a bit, he tells me. He would like to continue taking them.

I talk with my new psychiatrist. Grant should be sent elsewhere, a place where he can find the treatment he needs. We then find a program located in a remote part of the state with a sound reputation. They offer talking therapy with professionals. Outdoor activities are integrated into the process. Monitoring medication will continue. Tutors are available so as to help complete any school requirements. Living there alongside him will be other struggling teens for companionship.

As anyone might imagine this program is expensive. But what other option? Where would we find a thing, *anything*, on which to spend our money in the slightest way more important than helping our child.

He tells us he will not go. He runs away. He has walked out the school's front doors in defiance of the head of school and the school psychologist. These men, they had stood discouraged, troubled, as my son raced to get away from them despite facing suspension. This would be on his record, he had been told this. But they are not angry with him. Not in any way.

I guess where to look. He has met up with his oldest friend Brandon, the boy who had stuttered in grade school. He had gone looking for him at his school. Once the day ended, they had moved along to this boy's house.

I locate him there.

Robert and his grandfather go to collect him. An intervention is what is needed. He is tall, he is strong. He is angry. There is no physically "taking" him away. He says he wants to talk with his grandmother.

Once home his grandmother sits with him. She asks, "What are your options?"

He'll go back home, he'll return to school.

No longer on the table.

He will stay with them, his grandparents.

Not an option.

Brandon's family.

No.

He will get a job, his own apartment. He simply wants to be left alone.

"There is no job that will pay for an apartment." His grandmother explains this. "It will take three, maybe more, minimum wage paying jobs in order to do so." In other words, there will be no "left alone," there will exist no "hiding away."

As if possible to feel sadder than before, he is now profoundly, overwhelmingly, *terrifyingly* sad. But he will go off, now left with no further option.

His stay at home lasts a week or two longer, this after our intervention. He remains home since he contemplates attending his graduation ceremony.

But, just as before, during these days, he mostly doesn't get himself to school. Mostly I don't waste my breath. He stays in his room, alone. I too am alone. I hurt profoundly. Again I cry. I sit and I stare. At absolutely nothing.

In the end, and despite that he will not receive a diploma that evening, he does elect to attend the ceremony. Bravely he shows up, all the while knowing that, in its place, he will be handed a blank piece of paper. The school will accommodate him for these reasons: Because he is a good kid. Because he is loved, truly loved. Because all want the best for him.

Because he crushes them, tugs at their hearts.

He assures he will complete his work over the coming summer.

One five-page term paper must be written before a diploma will be granted him. This is what stands in his way of a certificate. And this is what has been standing in his way for three months. Despite the vastly competent, patient, eternally dedicated tutor at his side, this one paper has obstructed his path forward *for three lengthy months.*

As the ceremony nears he becomes more and more anxious. And too, he is anxiously conflicted. This is because he is fearful to be on stage in front of parents, grandparents, siblings, aunts, uncles, cousins, other students, teachers, administrators, people. Every bit of this exposure for two stabbing hours, during which (s)he will not be seen. And this devastates.

Yet he goes.

Albeit somberly.

As his hair is long, and although its curls spring upward, it yet extends a few inches beyond his shoulders. Sitting in the back row, he lowers his head and directs his hair to fall forward. This way he shrouds any possibility of exposing his face.

"Look up, please look up…"

He doesn't.

He can't.

He hurts.

Parker and I organize a "going away." This takes place a few afternoons following graduation, the day before Robert and I will drive him across the state. Many, many of his classmates show up. He has now made a 180 from middle school unpopularity. He is truly loved, respected. "*He's a nice kid.*" Parents of friends also attend. All greatly wish him happiness, contentment; they wish for him to heal.

He socializes, mingling among his peers for a while. Until he feels he can't. This is when he removes himself, walks off to his room, closes himself there. He lies down for a time before showing again. He is relieved when the party ends. Once more, always another time, I question whether I've done the right thing.

We leave early in the AM. The morning is dry, already warm. The drive will take six to seven hours. Occasionally we will cover lengthy stretches on long, one-lane roads. He lies down across the back seat and he sleeps. He is unresponsive and he is angry. He is sad and he is scared. Throughout the bulk of the trip the three of us are silent. The drive is painful. Leaving him will be unbearable. For us all.

I think of him then, as often I do: At birth, the first challenging time. I speculate continuously on where my happy, busy, interested-in-absolutely-everything child has gone. Going on seven years now my world has been a storm. A tsunami. But that which I do not yet know is that I have many additional years of the storm still to come.

We drive. I think. I cry. I sleep. I need to buck up.

As we step from the car, the program's director walks forward.

We meet the staff, a few other teens. We walk around the grounds. We're shown the individual huts, the yurt where meals are prepared, the community fire pit, the office. We walk three hundred or so steps to the river. The area is quiet, all pine trees and occasional open fields. It is warm and dry. It is peaceful.

In two hours it's time to leave him. His hug is lengthy and crushing. (S)he cannot, will not, let go of me, his/her weighty need of me continuous to consume every part of me. She embraces her father too. As we prepare to leave, her shoulders bend inward. Her expression is shattering, engulfing. Her face is misery itself. As we drive off Robert and I are empty, lifeless. Overrun by sorrow.

He stays six months, and so it is one week before Christmas when we pick him up. Parker comes along this time. Grant has spent Fourth of July, his birthday, and Thanksgiving away from us. We have talked very little during his stay, as per requested by the staff. For him, independence from family is crucial to moving forward. I send a pie through UPS on his birthday (really? it's all mush and soup when it arrives). When the box is opened, blackberries spill and stain all they touch. I send pointless candles, foolish party hats, asinine noisemakers. All for naught. As typical he doesn't wish for over-attention. How is it I do not yet know that?

Rule number one: No outside contact for two weeks. No computer ever. When letters arrive they will be censored by the staff. Any before-camp negative influences need to be addressed. Some of the attendees are battling drug addiction; others have been intermixed with gangs, intimidation, and violence. Mainly the mail Grant receives is from his two loyal friends. A few of his transgender mentors and, of course, there is contact with family: aunts, uncles, grandparents, brother. Us.

He is their puzzle, the staff's. The letters he receives are kind, nonthreatening. Every one. Agreeable people, well-wishers, those are the people who write to him. Those are his outside influences. They send support. Tell him about college classes, new friends, jobs. Ask when he's coming home. And then, seeing as he has no destructive outside attachments, the staff quickly deem it no longer necessary to read through his mail.

Grant is their favorite. They tell us this. He is kind, polite. He wants to sleep too much. He speaks with his psychiatrist via phone and his medications are upped. Even so, he wishes to sleep excessively often. As with us he speaks to no one about his dysphoria. Like us, the staff is baffled.

There is a young couple on staff who have a four-year-old. This child searches for Grant each morning. Knocks on his cabin door. They are pancake-making buddies. He follows Grant everywhere. Asks him to read to him. Sits on his lap. His mother joins them when they hunt for "keeper-rocks" at the river. Back in grade school Grant, as well as Parker, had taken cooking classes, week-long culinary "camps" that continued on for five sequential summers. As follows, their cooking knowledge, their love for the kitchen, all of this is expansive. Therefore Grant's skills are sought, appreciated, useful, and so he helps each evening with dinner preparation.

The summer is warm. The fall is dry. The attendees hike in a group with staff along, or one-on-one with a staff member. They bike on mountain trails. Raft the river. They talk. As promised there is a teacher on staff. Under her supervision Grant completes his term paper. His diploma is mailed to him with a thundering "*Congratulations!*"

As winter arrives they snowshoe. They talk, wait for mail. Cook. Read.

Grant makes one friend in particular, a girl. She is one year older than him. She had, for a brief time, been a meth user back home. She had mingled among the wrong crowd, a scary crowd. She is sensitive and kind. Troubled. But most importantly, her family cares and so she is there. She wants to be a chef, and she helps with dinner prep together with Grant. When he is not off with his four year-old-buddy or in counseling, he is with her. Sometimes the three are as one.

He corresponds with this girl throughout the following two years. I'm uncertain why this stops but, before it does, he learns she had begun chef school.

twenty-six

College Bound

He has accepted the offer of one of the two schools that had admitted him entry but had written in order to delay attending. This is one of the three schools that had received his application at 11:59 PM as miraculously he hit the deadline. He will attend this safety, second-choice school, winter quarter, the first of the year.

When January arrives he is passionate to be in school. Once more the math impresses all. Tests that are slated for an hour or more are completed in ten minutes, or less. But that which I don't yet know is that he barely makes this class. (But why would I be surprised?) He doesn't bother with any "meaningless" assignments between tests. (Why put myself out?)

As for me? Why waste energy on yet another elucidation…

That which I also do not know at this time, is that soon enough his depression comes back full strength. He seeks the school psychologist. He leaves his dorm room rarely, primarily for meals. Hardly ever for class. Any class. When back home spring break his English professor makes a stop at our neighborhood coffee shop. This is where she plans to meet up with Grant. Coach him along, encourage him to write. She knows he struggles. She has experienced his brilliance. So there emerges another, in his extensive list of adults, primarily women, who would like to help.

He is loved.

I will learn of all this "class avoidance," "depression," and "hand-holding" anew.

Eventually.

As the year ends his grades are dismal but he does pass. By a breath he achieves this. He won't share his grades with either his father or with me for obvious reasons.

Despite all his difficulties, however—poor grade trouble, his hiding away, his depression—he makes the decision to stay summer quarter. His mood has lifted somewhat due to the longer, brighter days, and too, he is determined to get this "throwaway" undergraduate study out of the way so that he can move on toward his master's and eventually his PhD. He desires a future. He tells us this. This is what we cling to.

The following fall he endures, he makes most of his classes. At the outset he does this. He doesn't show up every day but he does appear. Part time. Once more he struggles throughout winter when classes again are attended less and less often, until they are not. Until it's only a mid-term or an end-of-term exam that he shows for.

Or not.

The short, dark days are a challenge. Presenting as male is unbearable. In the end he narrowly passes the single remaining class he hasn't abandoned. This too is something about which we will need to wait years to learn.

The waiting.

The silence.

The silence…

twenty-seven

And There is More

I t is still too many years forward when we will learn of another significant challenge facing Grant, facing us…

Bipolar disorder.

In five years' time he will be diagnosed by the topmost doctor in our city, prominent in status and reputation, for the many years in his chosen field. He heads the psychiatry department at the University of Washington. He no longer sees patients on a regular, ongoing basis. In fact, he sees very few patients at all, and when he does…well, this is only once, a one-time shot, and then too, he will do so solely if the case is very severe. His purpose is to make recommendations to the patient's primary psychiatrist, psychologist, whatever be the case. He agrees to see Grant, likely due to my pleading, my urgency.

It is then, as soon as their hour together has passed, that he tells Grant he is bipolar. And he says this as well: *There has never been a time before this single sixty-minute session when he has made a diagnosis, one as serious as this one, in advance of many meetings spent.* But with Grant, he has identified right away that he is bipolar.

This atop all else.

Although, for now? Regrettably, it seems all the time regrettably,

I don't have insight into another crucial piece of the puzzle. This additional obstacle? This too is serious. But still I am unaware of even one thing that might help understand my child's suffering. Unremittingly I fail to navigate the maze that has become my life, I cannot find a way through the confusion. I cannot think beyond the chaos. I continue to stumble along. I zigzag about. I arrive nowhere.

twenty-eight

Deciding on the Best School

Amid family grief, confusion and turmoil, Parker has successfully, delightfully! made his way off to college. The application processes? These were a breeze. Maintaining steadily close to a cumulative 4.0, having taken multiple advanced level courses (this in an already challenging school where standard courses are known to be advanced by other schools' benchmarks), this combined with impressive SAT scores, he rightly applies to a handful of top-tier schools. He is engaged, enormously, in the course of action he will take. Robert flies with him around the country; they visit prospective schools. His first-choice school is one that chooses him as well. As in high school, as in middle school, just as in elementary school, he works hard, he succeeds, he is liked, *enormously loved. He is brilliant. He is a star*!

"Do you notice me now, Mom?"

"Dad?"

"Do you notice me now?"

twenty-nine

He Will Come
Back a New Person!

It is as soon as that second year in college has begun in full when Robert and I have another buzz of promise, a promise we hadn't felt since the summer of Grant's trip to France. When, *eagerly, zealously!* he went off to France. We now witness in him this same enthusiasm.

The finance company for which Robert works maintains its central office in New York, and it is in this city, at this company, where Grant would like to intern the upcoming summer. My psychiatrist tells me "He will come back a new person." This is the independence he needs (independence from us…from *me*). This will be the turning point, *the* point at which he will get on with his life. *The* point at which he will become a full "adult." He tells me I can expect this.

Grant looks for proper clothes, clothes befitting the job. Dressy attire. He wants my help with this. Okay, fair enough…he's a "guy," right?

While in New York he works in accounts receivable, busying himself with compiling bills and recording revenue. And then, it is as soon as his computer capabilities are revealed that he will troubleshoot any glitches the firm encounters.

He lives two days at a Midtown hotel until he moves into a room at the 92nd Street Y, until his summer residence there will be ready. And this particular Y, this is *the* Y. A *legendary* place. This owing to the exceptional concerts it hosts, the prominent literary events and dance performances that take place. Celebrated people who appear to lecture. This Y is a destination multicultural center. To stay here is a privilege, and this is where his father's company has secured him a room for the entire summer.

The office itself is situated on 42nd Street, and therefore, he will ride the subway linking Uptown to Midtown two times each day.

All this being in New York, this subway riding, this maneuvering about town, et cetera, this may not seem a big deal, and, of course, it isn't. Not for a person who has reached his age. But as known, he is not an average twenty-year-old. He is young. He has not proven independence. He isn't "tough." But he will work to navigate this immense labyrinth on his own. And he wants this. And…*"He'll come back a new person…finally he'll take command of his life!"*

There are times Robert will visit New York that summer. As it turns out, he shows at the office twice. While there, he takes Grant to lunch. To dinner. "All seems well," he reports. I don't contact him during his stay…anything to push the independence. And then also he doesn't call home. Good enough. In fact, perfect!

And too, while there he socializes with other interns. Never, not ever as much as the rest, but it's there. Restricted, but it's there…a social life.

Moreover he works hard.

He does this.

Again.

Until he doesn't.

Again.

Because this is the time, and this is the place, the phobias that have been building since high school take hold of him for real.

And the result of this? This amounts to spending early mornings in self-talk. He sweats, he shakes. His breathing is shallow. He wills himself to leave the room, but only half of these mornings does he succeed. He begins to show for work only part of the time. And the times he does manage he is likely, once more, to isolate himself from others. Secret himself away in an unused room. Again, neither his father nor I will know any of this. Until later.

Paris? This is one thing. New York? This is a harsher, faster thing. And then Midtown itself? This is *categorically unforgiving*. Midtown is *people*! Way too many people. People, unsmiling and forever hurried. People in your way, and you in theirs. Midtown, this is pushing and rushing…to catch a subway, secure a cab, sooner than the hurried person beside you. *Go*! Before the other secures it first! Midtown is transients, homeless souls, street vendors calling out. Imploring *you*! Midtown is people who are all business, businessmen and businesswomen, thousands and thousands of rushing professionals. It is multiple cultures and abundant languages, in one ear then around to reach the other. It is delivery trucks and standing cars. Midtown is *impatience*! It is drivers, drivers posed to rush a light, fixed to challenge your stepping from the curb. Midtown is *traffic*! and exhaust. It is fumes. It is ceaseless honking. Midtown is *noise*! It is filth. It is construction sites and closed-off sidewalks. Potholes. Bicycles weaving in and through. It is soaring buildings and it is shrouded sky. It is all this, and it is all the more.

And this is where Grant must show himself each and every day.

And this is where, and this is when, his phobias become unmanageable.

And so, as follows, on arriving back, he does not, in any manner, resemble the "well-on-his-way" sort of transformation I had been guaranteed.

thirty

Braving it Again

Yes, Grant *needs* school. He *wants* school. He *has* ambition. Still his greatest desire is to move forward. So he hides the terrors that had heightened and plagued him in New York, the best he is able. We wonder, worry whether he can make school work. But he needs this, profoundly and throughout he will not deny himself this. He goes off.

In the course of this quarter he meets a boy who seeks a house-mate. The two search for a modest place to live off campus. A tiny one-level duplex, somewhat dingy but clean, is what they find. It is a short two blocks off the main campus. His father and I bring furniture, dishes. We provide a bed. Sheets. Towels. He wants his childhood dresser, which we deliver. Although, by the time we have brought in this final item, he is anxious for us to leave. A panic attack is what he fears. Something he doesn't wish for us to witness. Something over which he doesn't wish to cause concern. His desire is to prevent our coming around too often. His need is to hide from the world, from us, *from himself (from me.)* that anything is wrong.

We place the dresser in his room, but by a whisper. We carry it just to the point where the door can open and close. And this is when fear overwhelms.

"Just leave it." This said hurriedly, nervously. The dresser is yet on an angle, still stretching too far into the middle of his undersized room.

"Let's place it against the wall. Out of the way," I offer.

"Just go." Now said with anger. With bitterness. Then, it is due to incapacitating depression, and debilitating anxiety, that he too cannot reposition his dresser more conveniently. His irritation, his resentment, this prevents us from future help as well. And therefore this is where his dresser remains for that entire year.

Throughout this period he continues to meet twice a week with the school psychologist. He is angry, very, at me. Their sessions are filled with talk of me, his anger, his *hatred* of me. I oppress him. He tells his doctor this. He says this to me later. I feel like I am a ball that two people, the two sides of him, use while playing catch. I barely pause in the hand of one, before I am tossed back into the hand of the other. *He needs me*! But too *I am in his way*! But then soon enough, *he needs* me. He wants my help, my support. He's mad (at me) because he needs me. He's mad (at me) because he wants my support. He's mad because he wants to break free of me. He's mad because I move to help. Because I lecture. Because I worry he will "fall down." Because I have seen him fall, over and over. Because he doesn't wish to disappoint. Because I worry he will hurt himself. Because I am scared. Because I am a mess too. (*Get yourself together, Sandra. Buck up! Model what you want. Just do it!*) I am tossed back and forth, back and forth, unendingly, back and forth.

Once again winter quarter is attended poorly. He sleeps a lot. He rises infrequently. For a second time he makes it through but, in the end, he is put on probation. Once more neither his father, nor I, are made aware of the severity of his depression, his fears, his probation. He is shameful of his depression. His fears continue to humiliate. As always he is unwilling to speak to us, to admit his "failings," and so he is silent. Always silent.

He stays through spring. Throughout summer. But by then his terrors have intensified ever further. His roommate is gone days on end. He is alone. He struggles to leave the house. But when we call he confirms all is well. We are not sure. We breathe.

We continue with our checking in. Our "making sure." Then, it is a month into the following spring when we cannot reach him. By this time his phone is turned off perpetually. He wants to be alone. He wishes to fade away. My psychiatrist tells me to give him space. But how? I worry for his life. I continue to call with no response. By the third morning I am on the road by 5:00 AM to make the trip north. I am terrified. By now, I am not simply emotionally sick; I am also ill physically. Due to blurry, tearful eyes I can *just* see through the windshield. The early morning is still, lifeless. As the sun rises traffic fills the road but I register no activity. The world is soundless. Motionless. Nonexistent.

When I reach his tiny rental I knock.

No sound.

The door is locked, bolted. I move around to the side and I pound on his bedroom window. This is when I hear movement, I think, but he keeps his voice silent, cautious. I shout out to him; I tell him it's me outside his room. This is when he makes his way to the door and opens up.

I look at him. He is defeated. Lifeless. He hasn't washed in days. His breath is foul due to no brushing, from continuous sleep. I hold him. I hold on to him for dear life. For his life, and for my own. I show as much strength as I am able but any bravado is false, a fleeting wave of relief. We take a short walk before he wants a meal. Over breakfast he says he wants to stay in school, he wants to study, he wants this so much. But he can't. He can't stay. He cannot study. And he needs me. Desperately.

This is when he admits he rarely leaves the house. By now he has stopped going to classes altogether. And he despises himself. His breath is shallow, he perspires, he shakes. Later I will learn that this is another time he must spend hours preparing himself, hours of self-talk, in order to reach an inward steadiness enough sufficient so that leaving the house may be possible.

This is what happens daily.

But he fails. He fails to reach the inner calm that would otherwise make going out possible, even for food. He spends days without food, unable to get to the grocery. We know nothing of this. As always he cannot explain the reason for all of this. He is tense, ashamed to admit he is afraid. So he doesn't reveal his panic attacks, his *fear of* his panic attacks. But his need to leave school, this is essential, vital. All the while he talks his legs shake uncontrollably, something of which he is unaware. "I need to come home. Please."

We head to the administration office. He withdraws from all classes. This complete withdrawal? This will be the first of three we will encounter. We pack his belongings, carry them to the car. I drive. He sleeps. He disappears into his room where he will remain throughout the course of the next two years.

thirty-one

A Week's Escape

Back when Parker was still in high school, the summer following his sophomore year, this during the six months Grant was away at "camp" in that remote area across state. The camp that would figure "'him' out," make him whole again. The summer Parker was living with us as an only child.

That summer?

That is also the summer Robert and I receive a phone call from the camp's director. "There is improvement," this he is eager to tell us. We, undoubtedly, are eager to hear this. Not without cause, Grant's improvement began the time he had received his high school diploma. "He is up." The director tells us this. "And has been so for weeks."

Robert and I are elated, buoyant. Permitting ourselves to soar all over again. And, as a result, we decide to take a trip. As in times before, we go to the mountains of Idaho.

Just Robert, Parker, and me.

In the course of our week away we bike a mountain trail, we swim and we float an icy river by way of tenuous inner tubes. We raft a river. We watch movies and we cook. We "hang out," the three of us. And although now sixteen, Parker doesn't seem to mind the absence of peers around him. Something that had often been part of earlier trips.

We stay in the town of Ketchum, a town the Big Wood River courses its way through. This is the river we tube. But the larger river, the Payette? This is located a couple hours' drive to the north, and this is the river we raft.

We head out early so as to get on the water by noon. This, so as to make time for breakfast along the way. And this meal is everything that is delightful abundance. Delightful *overabundance*. And in truth, it had been pre-planned to be just so, arranged to be a guilt-free, carb-plentiful meal of bliss: coffee and three thick, full-plate-size pancakes, butter, and syrup for Robert and for me; waffles with butter, three flavors of syrup, fresh fruit topped with whipped cream all combined with eggs, bacon, hash browns, juice, and toast for Parker, never-needing-to-count-a-calorie Parker…

The morning is cool, as typical for mountain climates, even in August. But by noon the temperature will reach eighty-five. By 1:00 it will be ninety. And this is good, needed, because this river, this is mountain ice and snow-melt-cold. Breakfast, this is conversation, lively and expectant. The drive is scenic. We point out wildlife, antelope, deer, a fox. There are steep peaks that surround us along the drive and, despite the August heat, although the many hot days that have since passed, up high there is still snow to see.

We reach the spot on the river to put in. The guide is there waiting. He informs that life jackets and helmets are required. The river ranges from class three to class four in difficulty. Or, in other words, class intermediate to class advanced. Although there is a point where the river will turn class six, the expert (perversity?) level. Here a rafter, a kayaker, must maneuver down a nearly forty-five-degree fall, all the while dodging boulders that rise to the surface. This is a fast decline. This is fast water. This is water in control. Control of your boat and in control of you. As follows, this requires immediate reaction, profound balance, and truthfully, a denial of the power of nature itself. Happily we sidestep perversity.

We raise the boat high above us as we climb the steep rock beside the fall and back down the jagged opposite other side. Once there we come across an aqua-colorful, thirty-foot deep, still pool that greets us. Immediately then Robert and I follow Parker back up the rise before we all take turns jumping from a height of maybe twenty feet. (And from this height, it is guaranteed that you will descend rather deeply. Therefore, from this height, it is certain that you will stay in the water (*ice and snow-melt.*) rather long. This is fun! No doubt! Absolutely! Our smiles are enormous!

I alone begin to shiver. I find a protective layer, which is not thin. And as I am really, quite cold from my *three foolish leaps* into the "liquid ice," and despite the ninety-degree air, I wish, in fact, I had brought more, quite a lot more, protection.

Another pool awaits us as our float resumes. And this pool, this is also still…once inside. But outside? Outside is angry, churning white water. On the far side of the pool is smooth rock rising endlessly skyward. And "this place," our guide informs, "is where boats flip." More often than not.

Naturally Parker wants in, as does Robert. Despite they *see* my shiver, no matter they *hear* my chattering teeth, they want this *for me, as well*!

So yes, I'm back in the water. And yes, they both want back

inside this pool two more times…, but afterward, at the end of our two-hour float, once we have arrived at the take-out, once my skin is sunbaked and my teeth rest still, I am indeed happy we have taken this trip. I am happy to be with Parker, *as an only child*.

A few days following is the afternoon we decide to bike a mountain trail. And this day is also hot. Hot, dry, and dusty. For the most part as we ride there are no trees and therefore there is no shelter from the rising heat nor the blinding glare of the midday sun. (Why did I come?)

…Oh yeah. Family time.

Parker time!

Then too, aside from the heat, the dust and the glare, there is yet one more disagreeable aspect that plagues this trip, for me: I don't know my bike. I don't know the difference between what the right handle brake controls versus the brake shift on the left. I, in fact, don't know this opposite handle, specific brake problem even exists. And so, as I slow down on this trail, this trail that Parker and Robert have enthusiastically agreed upon, a trail which is really quite narrow (really, why so narrow? Why so uneven? Why the loose rock? Why so many impatient bikers approaching from behind? Why the elevation gain? Up and down and *up*!) and so as I slow to avoid careening off the slope that threatens to my left, I squeeze the brake that controls the front tires.

Not the back tires, not the "preferred" both-of-them tires. No. That is a thing I do not do. And therefore it is immediate when the bike pitches forward only to hurl me, or rather, *somersault me*, over its handle bars. This is what it does, this bike I don't know. This bike I no longer want to know.

And the result of all this pitching and flinging? I begin to do just what I had feared: I careen down the slope, this slope with its dirt, dusty-red. Rocks, pointy-sharp. Its shrubs, prickly and haphazardly arranged.

I slide a good fifteen feet. My bike slides maybe three. As for Robert and Parker? They are way up and around the turn ahead, not once checking behind. (*Thank you!*) I lift my scratched, filthy, bloody self as far as a crawling position and inch my way back up.

Now pushing this bike (I don't like), I proceed again. At times flattening myself against the dirt wall on my right to avoid the "get out of the way already" riders aplenty who surprise from behind.

I walk. I press on, I plead with the brake system before I brave pedaling again. Robert and Parker wait twenty minutes at the opposite trailhead before Parker, having endless energy, volunteers to pedal back up. He rides enough distance so that another twenty minutes pass before we meet up. Despite my scrapes, my pain, my bloody knees and hands, when I see him, I laugh. After his initial glance, once he sees that I am "having fun," he laughs too.

Okay, maybe that was a certain *type* of fun? A torment-your-body *kind* of fun? An *I-am-so-very-happy-it's-over form* of fun?

Truthfully, it is exactly what Parker has classified "*Type-Two Fun*"…

It is the winter following this trip when the father of a friend of Parker's tells Robert and me something that mattered, *matters, a lot*. Parker, he had talked about the week the three of us had spent together the previous summer. He expressed then it had been the best vacation he'd ever had.

I think that over. I consider our previous times away: Disneyland when Parker was five, riding the Matterhorn, floating through the pirates of the Caribbean, both rides taken over and over at his delight. The trip to Paris where we spent hours inside the Napoleon War Room at Les Invalides, a guided tour he never wanted to end. I consider all the trips to Hawaii where we snorkeled, where Parker and Grant had worn themselves out in the waves with boogie-boards. All family ski vacations. The Oregon Coast. Ziplines and fishing. The Statue of Liberty, Central Park, the view from atop the Empire State Building…et cetera, et cetera, and vacation et cetera…

But *this* is what he had said: his *best vacation. Ever.* Although still in my profound mother confusion I, as of yet, am unable to grasp the significance of his words. Still I am not capable of comprehending how much he craves our attention. Needs us. *Needs me.* Still I am unable to appreciate how much neglect I have been guilty of.

thirty-two

Holding Pattern

Grant's stay at home progresses. This after his time at the rental. Eventually I learn of the inner battles he had endured while in New York, the showing up for work only part of the time. He can no longer keep this from me, from his father. Although, I am still incapable of understanding what all this means. I realize it is owing to severe unhappiness, but it is an unhappiness that eludes me, depression that confuses. I know *only* about the depression, the anxiety. Nothing else.

And as I try to understand, when I probe, he again masks his fear behind anger. Outwardly. With stubbornness. Both provocative and incendiary. Directed at me. Always at *me*. *I* am his continuous target. I can see nothing beyond his anger, his obstinacy, which eventually turns to silence. I know not a thing about phobias so, all combined, I am unable to detect what is truly going on. But what *is unquestionably* going on are indeed phobias, profound and insurmountable fears. So what began as severe social anxiety in high school, then grew impossible in New York, has now become full-blown terror. And in short time, this agoraphobia, it will progress into the pan phobia that will debilitate still beyond. Yet his terrors remain something he will not disclose, something he will continue not to disclose, until too much time has been wasted, until too many battles have been fought.

As continuously, rather than offer explanation, he persists in focusing off and away. Ceaselessly away. And while doing so he continues uncompromisingly to place the screen before him. Of course he does this while hiding away in his room. His sole safe place. His haven. His *asylum...* As I continue to lack any knowledge of what to do.

Incessantly I remain terrified he will take his life. There are more doctors, more upping of dosages. We are way beyond high school level of isolation.

A few months pass. I am angry at life. I am beaten. I am *shattered*. And I am worn by Robert's too-often times away. More and more I cannot keep up with Grant's profound needs. Not on my own. And, just as in earlier days, there are occasions when his silence, his *unrelenting stillness*, will again spur in me an anger that takes absolute claim over me. And these are the moments, into hours, that any compassion evaporates. Entirely.

But I don't want to harass him. I don't wish to be that mother. I *try* not to harass him.

Who is the mother I have become? How did everything I had hoped for unravel before me? How is it that an understanding of how to mend my family remains so far out of reach? So far out of *my* reach...

I am the mother I never wanted to be.

And I harass...

"Get up! Get out of the house! Do *something*! What is wrong with you?" This time said as reproach. I fluctuate between my desire to annihilate him and my "mother bear" instinct to coddle him. In every way I am so very mixed up.

My words, not unexpectedly, have their negative effect. "What goes around comes around," this is especially true when the one pressing back is so overwhelmingly distraught. Think barely hanging on.

So my reproach is met with door slamming, calls to his father (tattle-telling on Mom). Hiding further away. Verbal abuse: "You are a bitch! I'm never enough for you! You make me sick! You are a failure of a mother! *Get away from me*! *I wish you were dead*!"

His verbal retaliations are unquestionably immature, another thing I heatedly point out to him. "Grow up already." In (now three) more years I will understand the reason for this too. Because it is once I learn (s)he is transgender that I will hit the books, I will talk with other parents of transgender young adults. Again, frustratingly I must wait until that time to become enlightened as to the cause of all this childishness. Only then will I discover that it is the age when a person deeply admits to themselves they are, without doubt, in the wrong body, even though they still may not understand what any of this means, that they stop moving forward emotionally. Rarely is this without exception.

Mercifully, however, with time this will work itself out.

His/her pause in emotional growth will cease to continue as soon as she begins to make the change. All the same, this gap between age and emotional maturity, this will be a gradual working out. It will take several more years before the gap will close completely. Too many years before she will be able to "act her age." His/her actual age is twenty-one. But for now I proceed in making more mistakes as I have no idea I am currently dealing with a twelve-year-old.

Moreover, just as in previous times, during these motionless years, he cannot make his doctor appointments, not on his own. So I drive him. Two, sometimes three times a week, I drive him. And I linger nearby, in a coffee shop, in a lobby, a waiting room, for the sessions to be over. Reading for me has now become pointless. I stare at passages without awareness. It is over and over that I repeat the same pages without absorbing one piece of content. Each hour I linger feels to be decades as continuously he consumes my every thought. My entire life. Every aspect of my being is perpetually on hold.

And, again, all this stolen attention, this relentless "holding pattern," this is to the injury of Parker. Is it his turn yet? Will it *ever* be his turn? Chaos and guilt, despair and helplessness, chaos and guilt.

A year goes by. No change. This is when I begin to stay out of the house as much as possible. I cannot bear the oppressive. The weight of the oppressive. The stillness of his sleep. The incessant quiet. The nothingness. My own depression is acute. My fear is stabbing, again threatening my sanity. This is another time when friends call and I don't return their efforts. Again they give up. I don't know where to place myself. Public spaces are difficult. Another coffee shop? Occasionally…then, how often? How long? can I sit unable to distinguish what's in front of me? How much coffee can I tolerate? Often I am inside my car parked just down the street sleeping and crying and screaming. Pounding the steering wheel, hammering the dash. And, all over again, I sleep.

Eventually it arrives to the period that he has locked himself away for a year and six months. Eighteen months of solitary confinement. He is fading away emotionally and physically. Visibly and literally he is dying.

And this is the time he develops the cough. A serious cough. A fever, high. Our family doctor is needed. Inevitably he has developed pneumonia. He has developed this by way of lying on his back without pause, by lying prone in general, he maintains this flat-out position while he sleeps. Fretfully, fearfully he sleeps. Or while on his computer. His mindset a void.

At the doctor's office he is given a full examination. Something he has avoided (refused to do) for two years.

But now he realizes he must and so I take him. And again I wait around in a coffee shop. *Another coffee shop.* I am tired, fed up with waiting. And what is more, afterward, after my ninety-minute wait, he offers not one word as concerns his checkup. Not one word. As usual, this is what he does. As usual this is what he does *not* do.

And so all over his silence incenses me. Infuriates me. "*I do so much for you.*" He doesn't care. He is mad that I do so…that he feels I must do so.

Our family doctor calls that afternoon. "Grant has gained too much weight." He has done so, of course, owing to no activity. Owing to anxiety and depression. Due to phobias. Worry over a hidden identity. He eats in order to suppress his angst. His agony. He eats as solace. I am reluctant to reveal too much of his sloth-like existence. (*Start to parent effectively, Sandra. Buck up. Set a proper example.*) Our doctor informs that Grant has now developed borderline type II diabetes. This as well. And the reason I receive this call? The reason our *doctor* must tell me this? This is because Grant is fearful to talk of his pneumonia, of the full-blown diabetes that threatens. He is anxious over my "I told you so," my own anxiety, my helplessness and my sense of futility.

So our doctor has agreed to relay his diagnoses to me at Grant's request. Exasperatingly for me he knows that Grant is unwilling to confide in me, to trust in me to do the "right" thing. Our doctor imparts this as well, as if to say, "Go easy on him." He informs me then that Grant must lose the extra weight. He must lose sixty pounds. He recommends a hospital nutritionist which Grant agrees to see. He is afraid over his health. I can see this. I am anxious he will need to take ever-more medication in order to barely survive. He understands this as well. He is motivated… so he *does* care whether or not he lives? Having witnessed his concern, I desperately, albeit feebly, cling to this notion.

Following his prescribed diet, he progresses to lose ten pounds each and every month forward so that in six months' time he not only feels healthier, he *is* healthier.

Physically.

He wants my approval over this.

He despises himself for wanting my approval.

He despises me for wanting my approval.

He despises *me* for this.

He retreats to his room…

thirty-three

Shame

The result of all this crushing "non-life," this anger and discouragement, there emerges another something. And this "*something,*" this is something of which the memory haunts me, because the memory is as cruel as the thing itself. It will follow me everywhere and it will remain part of me always. And this *something?* This is the most shameful act of my life.

Can it be that everyone has "*one,*" *the* action that stands out as "*it,*" as the most reprehensible? Most disgraceful? A thing intolerable?

It is now nearing two years into this current hiatus at home. Four years into Grant's agoraphobia. And by this time, over two years have been swallowed up by pan phobia as well. Over two years, *four years,* all during which time evaporates. For us all. For him. For me. As customary, primarily for the two of us. A fear of *everything?* I hadn't known this existed. Not until I experienced it in my child, not until his doctor labeled him as such, as pan phobic.

Imagine a fear of sleeping. Of adjusting the radio. Of the three- and five-year-olds who live next door. Imagine breaking into a sweat, shaking with no control or a gut ache so intense you must curl yourself inward. Imagine at minimum one, perhaps all of these occurring multiple times a day. Every day. For years on end.

Then imagine yourself watching all this and being unable to help. And I don't understand the reason I cannot help, the reason I cannot make a difference. But, again, as I will later discover, at its core is his fear over a hidden identity, likely exasperated by bipolar disorder. But still I haven't knowledge of either. And therefore I am not simply helpless, I am meaningless.

Moreover, as I cannot understand this illness that emerges as defiance, noncooperation and resentment directed at me, I am *angry. Endlessly angry.* And it will be years before I do understand. Years before I will come to realize that he truly cannot clean up the messes he makes…in the kitchen, in the bathroom, throughout the house. It will be years before I will understand there exists an actual sickness that will prevent him from changing his sheets or doing his laundry, from showering. From leaving the house.

But as I am without this knowledge, I am *furious* for the work I do for him. For him, my twenty-two-year-old grown child, I must continue to do *his* cleaning, *his* grocery shopping, *his* slog. I am angry that his presence is leaden, a darkness. Everything that is hopeless.

I am angry.

And I want him to realize that he is shattering me, that he is destroying me. I wish for him to know that I am dying too.

So it is with this in mind, this permeating the entirety of me, that I act. But this act, this is without premeditation. This is simply an act of desperation. Of despair. This is sheer passion.

It is early evening. Again I am in tears while I speak, while I attempt to beget reason. "Please get up." He lies on his bed, as habitual he simply lies there. "Please *do something*. Can't you see what you're doing to yourself, to me…to us?" My voice vacillates between one that is highly raised and one that is barely audible. My angst, my grief, these are wholly without containment.

He's up now and he's yelling back. "*Go to hell! Everything is always about you, isn't it Mom? Leave me alone! Stop harassing me! Go away!*" His voice reverberates with the volume and the potency of it. With his misery and with his rage.

I turn away next and leave the room. Overpowered, overwrought.

I step into the bathroom and close the door. I am crying. Hard. Profoundly and without end, I sob. I reach into the cabinet for an Advil PM. I need to go to sleep. I need for my life to disappear. *I* need to disappear. Everything about this unmanageable world needs to vanish. I wish to evaporate. Dissolve. Waste away. I wish to die.

He opens the door in his fury and he begins to shout again, but then he stops himself. I have taken hold of the container of Advil PM; I pitch my head backward and that is when I empty the entire contents into my open mouth. *See what you're doing to me? Can you see it now?* Those are the words my actions tell.

All the while the back of my throat is closed off, but he doesn't know this. And next I lean in and begin to spit out the pills until I get rid of every one, until the sink is filled with the entirety of them. And I believe he has witnessed this. But he hasn't. He doesn't see this because he's already run for the phone. But I don't know where he's gone. I don't realize why he's left. Although now that he's away, I take my one pill, the amount I had intended to take all the while. And I go to bed.

I'm in bed maybe ten minutes when my bedroom door opens. Standing above me are two medics. And there are two police officers who accompany these medics. Their pistols are out.

I will learn the reason for the presence of the police later. Their guns at the ready. Where there is threat of suicide, I discover, there is often domestic abuse at its side. Their presence is simply protocol.

I am put on a stretcher despite my pleas otherwise. Despite that I confess to ingesting only one pill. And I say this over and over to deaf ears. I am sobbing again. I do not look stable and, of course, I am not stable, but too, I have taken simply one pill. I want to go back to my darkened room where I will be alone with my grief, where soon all will pass away in sleep.

Grant is crouched, huddled against the lower cabinets in the kitchen as I am carried past him and through the room. He too is sobbing. And he is shaking.

Outside I see squad cars, three in all, with overhead flashing lights. The additional officers, guns out as well, escort the medics, me, to the waiting ambulance and I'm taken away.

Grant reaches Robert by phone. All this has transpired during a short trip to the grocery. So, once informed, Robert hunts down my whereabouts, which is the mental branch of a local hospital. This is where I wait, on a braked gurney in an overly crowded, overly lit hallway among rushing doctors and hurried nurses. Among other patients laying atop stationary gurneys. Among the cries and the shouts and among the weeping. This is the spot where Robert discovers me.

Two hours pass in the hallway before I am wheeled into an examination room where I will speak with a psychiatrist. This doctor then informs me I will stay through the night where I can be watched over, monitored. "If I had swallowed the pills wouldn't I be showing signs?" I impart this to the doctor. "I'm fine." Robert confirms this. But he wants to know one earthly reason I would fake an attempt of suicide.

I cannot answer the question, my shame being too immense.

He tells me he will not grant my release unless there exists a reason for this act, one that he can comprehend. He needs to believe I will not hurt myself after I've left.

Then. I tell him. With unbearable shame, I say this: "I wanted my son to realize that I hurt. I didn't think. I simply acted." And then too, "I believed he had witnessed my getting rid of the pills. I thought he knew all was okay."

The outcome of this? The painful, demoralizing aftermath of my confession? (The one of three devastating results of my *act*?) This doctor, he stared at me with more aversion, more loathing than ever I had experienced before. Next, raising his hand in disbelief: "Get out of my hospital" is the only thing he said before leaving the room.

And the added two consequences? One is the forever shame I will carry with me. And the last and most important cost? This is the terror I put my child through during a time his fight for survival was nominal, at best.

thirty-four

New Doctor

I describe Grant's behavior, his life (*his non-life*), to my own doctor in lengthier, greater depth. This is when I learn he must begin to see a cognitive therapist. A *cognitive therapist. This* is now needed. *Too. This*, in addition to his psychiatrist. His psychologist. (Deny treatment? If only…)

The money we spend is *daunting*.

The cognitive therapist is essential, I am told, to battle the phobias clearly plaguing him. The psychiatrist? This in order to prescribe his many needed medications. The psychologist, this is someone extra. We will continue to allow these sessions simply to accommodate Grant. He tells us this doctor feels to him significant in abetting his process forward.

As one understands then, there are *a lot* of appointments. *A lot* of obligations. *A lot* of time spent. For the both of us.

During the time he begins to see this new doctor he makes contact with our former sitter. This is after twenty-two months at home have passed. It is June. Our sitter, she is trusted. She is a rock, a needed and much-applauded tower of strength. To us both. And too she loves Grant, she loves both my "sons." She suggests that Grant come live with her for a few months' duration. And so he does. Gratefully he does this. He wants away from me. From my sermons, my tears. His need of me. Desperately I want away from him too. Throughout his time there he pays for food out of the money he had over-earned while in New York. Money he was given despite all the eventual non-performance that came to be.

The hours our sitter spends at work, however, Grant continues to hide away. He fears everyone. Everything. The summer days are bright. He draws the shades over each and every window. He isolates himself in the dark. He "lives" in the stillness of the house; he "exists" in the emptiness. He survives by willing an all-invasive numbness.

I go around to pick him up the three times a week he must show at his appointments. His endless appointments. His countless doctors. When I arrive, every time I arrive, he is ill. His stomach hurts. His head aches. He thinks he may have a fever. He lowers his head as he walks toward the car. I am fearful to "push" him too hard, afraid to thrust him into an ever more overwhelming place. I will leave all this to his doctors.

So I continue to listen to this "sick-talk." I continue to do too much for him. I continue to believe I must do too much for him. Later, once I am able to speak with his psychiatrist, I will learn I have been going about things the wrong way, yet again, because as known, doing for him only serves to feed my anger. Doing for him only serves to feed his anger.

And as far as *his* anger? This, without doubt, only serves to advance my sense of hopelessness, my interminable exhaustion. But until I come to learn otherwise…before I realize that all my help *denies*, not *encourages*, his moving forward…I will continue to "help" because, at my core, I remain fearful he will take his life if I do not.

He is rude to me. Only to me is he this way. But he is rude because he is sick. And he is my child so I will work endlessly to change this.

In the course of his newest appointments he and his added doctor spend time engaged in conversation, but of greater importance, they spend time venturing out into the world. These excursions, this "*real-life practice*," I learn, is the defining praxis separating cognitive therapy from other therapy forms.

The doctor's office is situated in the core of downtown. From this spot the two "take on" the outside world. Under the watchful eye of his doctor, initially placing herself just a step away, Grant must make purchases, ask strangers for directions and then too… he is required to do something foolish; he must brave embarrassing himself in front of others. The goal is to allow the patient to realize they can, and *will*, survive all this external pressure. The goal is for the patient to appreciate that no one nearby is paying too much attention, if at all, to anyone within their surroundings, foolish or not. Because, in all honesty, people rarely grant attention to anything other than their own happenings, to anyone other than their own selves.

With each consecutive session they visit various locations and, all the while, as Grant performs these requirements, his doctor proceeds to situate herself farther and farther away. They take bus rides across town. At the outset, as in other circumstances, the doctor places herself on the seat beside him. Then, subsequently,

she distances herself until eventually they sit in opposite locations, one at either end of the bus.

He braves through. He breathes. This cognitive therapist, she
has taught him to engage his mind when he feels fear invading.
"Thinking," she says, "is key." Crucial. This as opposed to allowing sheer emotion to override. "Think, focus your way through."

He works at this. Sometimes he succeeds. And the times he
succeeds? This is another time I allow myself a brief, desperately
needed, moment of calm.

All these sessions, this encouragement and confidence building,
this is good. Helpful. But too, as concerns significant progress?
All this is slow going. Nevertheless, by the time he is impatient
to return to school *some* strides, if only slight, have been made.

thirty-five

Exposure

All during this past summer, this past fall and now winter, Grant has resumed sessions with the same university psychologist he has consistently seen. By now they have an established, trusted relationship. Grant is worried about me. And again his talk is predominantly of me. He describes to this doctor the episode with the Advil PM, the mental ward of the hospital where I had been taken. Now there exists one more person who knows of this shameful event, every detail. But due to immense disgrace, that night is something about which I have not yet spoken with my own doctor. I tell myself I will do so. Eventually. It's just that…well, I'm waiting for the right moment…

Moreover I have no idea any of this incident has been recently discussed beyond our immediate family. But now, since Grant fears I will take *my* life, just as I fear he will take *his*, his need to talk is urgent.

Implicit is the mess I have created is formidable. It has drawn both of us further downward. This is a deep hole, an abyss that recklessly and terribly I alone have thrown us into.

The two doctors then talk. His psychologist has contacted my own, and the news of my disgrace has been passed along.

I am caught. The spotlight is glaring, blinding. No longer can I withhold my shameful doings from the world. No longer can I hold them at bay from myself. No more can I avoid my doctor's scrutiny. And then, that which I had anticipated comes to be, because my doctor, he shows no compassion. His reaction is the same as was the doctor's the night of the nightmare. And so I sit silently, and I sit stiffly, facing my doctor, "facing" myself, as he proceeds to "beat me up." *But never mind Doc, I already do that. Every single day.*

Now that all my garbage, my indignity, my consequences have been hurled about me. Flung at me. What's left? Well, I must talk to myself for real. And if nothing more, I will work to heal within. And, more importantly, I will be fierce to eliminate this added distress from my child.

thirty-six

Bipolar

Despite his braininess, or rather due to the make-up of his brain itself, bipolar continues to derail. Because bipolar... this is serious. And bipolar, this is complex. It can manifest itself in varying ways and change up without warning. *Surprise*! You are agitated! You do not make sense! *Newsflash*! You cannot move.

Bipolar can be the cause of paranoia likely followed by social withdrawal. It can be the source of withering to nonexistent self-confidence. Bipolar is confusion and an unsettling neediness. It is erratic, unhinged behavior.

And so without proper medication to battle the inevitable chaos, it can be all of this irrepressibly. It can be all of this incomprehensibly.

I, as of yet, have not received the diagnosis.

Although in truth, "this" *is* familiar because on a reduced scale this illness is also part of me. But due to the diminished level, I can manage my symptoms without much effort. As for Grant and owing to the distance that separates the degrees of our illness, his behavior is yet bewildering, as there are days in succession when he is awake, his head abuzz. These episodes, they can carry on up to *three* days. *Or longer*. There, in fact, *have been* times when seventy-two hours have transpired for my son, seventy-two hours while his brain holds him captive…seventy-two hours without the ability to sleep. Three solid days in his room, exasperatingly awake, and on his computer.

And next? Next is the inevitable switch. And therefore, as his "hyper" begins to abate, his exhaustion emerges. (*When one then always the opposite other.*) And this exhaustion, this is noteworthy. Without dispute, this is understandable. So just as in his manic confusion, there are days without break while he sleeps. In his room. Sequestered away. Unmoving.

thirty-seven

Honing Skills;
Replacement for a Social Life

By the end of this same spring we discover Grant's emotional depletion has again returned. Anxiety has weakened any former sense of reserve he had worked so hard to maintain in order to fight his terrors. And, as follows, agoraphobia reveals itself once more and heartlessly takes hold.

He comes home. This is the second of the three intervals to date he will do so.

As expected, he, his room, and his computer re-establish their never-coming-up-for-air relationship. In all ways they are an immersion of one, a bonded, blurred nonentity. And, just as in earlier times, he spends his time playing games, followed up with playing games, followed up with… But too, all the while he does this, he analyses the strategy intrinsic in them. He studies both the strategies used in the creation of these games as well as the strategy used in order to defeat them. He unmasks codes.

And, owing to this dedication, or rather, due to his *fixation*, *his obsession*, *his addiction*, he is put in position to further his relationships online. And this "online relationship furthering," this, he believes, is a social life. He tells me as such. Of course, as avowed, this "socializing" is primarily with other "gamers," but also he corresponds with the creators of these games themselves. To these individuals he makes suggestions on how to improve code and how to progress strategy. He gives advice on ways to secure against shortcut players or unforeseen cheating schemes. He shares his observations, his awareness on how to improve efficiency. He is able to provide this insight by way of his inherent knowledge of game strategy. And it is this knowledge that is further honed by time spent playing and evaluating. The games' creators, they deem his input useful. They welcome his correspondence. They learn valuable, in-depth knowledge of their own games, from *him*.

There exists one well-known game in particular. A game that is extensively popular, thrilling to many, and equally to Grant himself. In truth, this game is the most sought, most played game to date, with well over one hundred million players worldwide. He writes to the creators of this phenomena. To them he offers twelve suggestions for improvement.

They implement every one.

He is smart.

At least he is very smart…

thirty-eight

Breaking Through

It is now six months at home this current period when I ask, I *tell*, I *demand*: "I need to talk with your doctor."

He, as always, remains silent. So next I plead. I *beg*. "Please let me know how to help you?" I promise, I swear to him, "I will not inquire about the issues you two discuss," something I have said over and over. My endless, boundless badgering of him. "I simply want direction. I need to know my role, even one way I may provide help ..."

But his fear of my discovery, the unknown of my response, these terrors run deep. They are as frightening to him as the prospect of death itself. *Death by way of rejection.*

But, despite all odds otherwise, this is finally the time he fights back his fears and *does* give permission. This doctor, she is bound by law to adhere to Grant's demands so no, she will not discuss their sessions, the content of them. She consents to communicate a way in which I may be of help. Period.

Okay. I'll take even a crumb.

She calls in one day, gives me the name of another cognitive therapist who has an office within the larger practice of which she is a part. It is within seconds of our conversation that I make the call. My first appointment, with Robert along, is the following week.

As we arrive for our initial session we quickly learn that this doctor will work with us as a "behaviorist," part of the cognitive approach. His goal is to help direct the two of us on how to go about our parenting in order to obtain the behavior we seek from Grant.

This then is the time we learn Grant is now an age where we do not have to accept his refusal to do that which he has no desire to do. There are ways around this. Moreover, we can achieve this without yelling, without beating him into a fragmented speck. We can do this. But we must manipulate the situation smartly. We cannot bend toward "*easy*." We will back him against an unwavering wall. Even if his booming voice, his frantic yelling (a given) occurs. And we must continue with this "*unwavering*" as a means uninterrupted. This is what we must do, despite my continued worry that pushing him too hard will thrust him irretrievably over the edge, even though I fear for his life in doing just that.

So, for me, *this is not easy.*

This, in fact, *is something miles beyond not easy.* I feel small. Terrified. Sick. But our doctor says what we will do, this is imperative. Crucial. What we will do, this is tough love.

And so we do it.

He has one week then, seven short days, to find a job, a class, or volunteer work. One week before he will be forced to find a new place to live…even if this place is on the streets. Period. In addition, it will be mandatory to be out of the house eight hours each day. The only concession is Sunday. Unyielding again.

Then too, if his job, class, or volunteer work will be less than full time, he will need to find someplace to pass the additional hours. And so this becomes law. His "no-way-around it," unnegotiable, set-in-stone law.

Five days pass while he searches, scrambles to discover something with which he can occupy his time. Fill his eight hours. He begins to panic.

But next, it is the sixth day when he visits his former high school. He makes his way to the theater and this is where he locates his former teacher who creates and builds set designs, something he had loved doing during his "happier" moments there. He offers his help as a volunteer. And this instructor, he says yes. Definitively *yes*!

And so he does it. Amid formidable fear, he doesn't break down and he makes the deadline. As for me? Once again I search for air.

thirty-nine

College Suits Him

Parker continues along in glowing success. College suits him. Carleton College suits him. A college only the best and hardest working are given entry. While there, he receives academic awards, one after the other, for his distinction in chemistry, as a student who achieves excellence in the sciences.

He is granted one award in particular, an award that is vastly prestigious in the sciences and bestowed to only a handful of the topmost undergraduate students across the nation. He graduates Sigma Xi and Phi Beta Kappa from this school. The first indicating significant research in the sciences. The latter as one landing within the top five percent of his graduating class.

He receives admiration from professors, both on campus and while studying abroad. He travels to Australia where he spends a semester attending classes as well as providing research in the university's lab. The professor under which he studies offers him a position if he were to return to continue his study in this same program during his postgraduate years.

He likes the outdoors, Parker. No, he *lives* for the outdoors. Sports and recreation, too often teetering toward the extreme for my comfort. While in Australia he becomes a certified scuba diver.

It will be later when he will travel to the Bahamas with the scuba team from a neighboring college. Willingly this school allows him to join, this despite never before having been approached by an off-campus student. He is *resourceful*, he is *loved*, and he is *admired* immensely. He is all of this. Continuously so. Extraordinarily so. While in Australia he takes up skydiving, and although his father learns of this quickly, I am thankfully not informed until many years have passed. Until Australia is a distant memory. Until he has returned…until he is safe, and he is sound. In the US.

He joins his school's mountaineering club. In a year's time he will be elected as its president. It is also during this time that he decides he will climb the highest peak on each and every continent. *This* is his goal.

This is my ever-mounting anxiety.

After graduation he spends the summer rock-climbing, mountain biking, river kayaking. When fall arrives he settles himself in a northern state on the East Coast where previously he had secured a job on a lobster boat. He is determined to experience the larger world. He works hard. He stays occupied at this until the first of December, until the waters become too wild. Too unpredictable. Too cold. Until the warmer, calmer season of "lobstering" has ended.

And this is when he drives the thousands of miles back to the west. Not all the way west, not home. Rather, he spends the remainder of that school year in a mountain town, not our adopted mountain town but, rather, an "undiscovered" town, with an unfamiliar mountain. One that will provide further exploration, further familiarity, with yet unknown parts.

Although, while there he will endeavor no resort skiing…no,

he will simply "skin ski." He will bond narrow strips of manufactured animal skins to the bottom of his skis, skins that will adhere to snow while walking uphill. Then he will ascend peaks unprotected and unmonitored by the neighboring resort...unprotected and unmonitored by the ski patrol inside the boundaries of the neighboring resort. This is what he does with the handful of new friends he makes while there. In his free time, when not at work in the restaurant where he has found employment for the season, he does this.

And yes, my anxiety?

No, this doesn't pause. Rather it climbs, it mounts, it ascends. Until it conquers.

forty

Enlightenment at Last

F all has arrived another time. Grant will try school once more and he settles into his newest dorm. He is twenty-four. He is fourteen. His dorm-mate is eighteen.

Moreover, in combination with these age disparities, the two simply live in diverse worlds, marking an impossible coming together. The two as one? It would be easier discovering sunlight in a cave.

And too, added to the intrinsic dissimilarities between them, this personality incongruence which unavoidably separates, it is now that our daughter/son has begun to embrace her true identity. Both inwardly and outwardly she does this. And this she does with friends she's made on campus, with beloved professors. And this she does within her dorm. She begins to wear nail polish. Girlfriends take her to the mall to hunt for clothes…this carries little success, though, given her height. They find scarves, headbands. Additional shades of polish.

The boy with whom s(he) shares a room is a different sort. A football enthusiast, a devotee to all things athletic. It would be that sports are his chosen "religion." So he is a tough guy. A "man's man." My daughter describes him to me this way. And she feels to be locked inside a prison together with this boy, both in turn captives who must divide space within a tiny, airless cell. He has placed a large television at the foot of his bed, this cellmate. This television is turned on, volume up. Continuously. He watches football. He watches basketball, sports! Talk shows concerning sports. He has a long-time aversion to the LBGTQ community. This is what my daughter tells me. This is how she defines her confinement with him.

So she remains out of the room as much as possible. This she does as much to avoid her roommate, as the incessant television, and the noise of it.

Then, as would be foreseeable, each are fraught to be sprung from this cruel arrangement in which they have been forced to live. Side by side. And so each pleads with the school for early release. Which they are then granted.

So my sensitive, now-mollified daughter stays in the room they once shared, while her television-fevered, sports-zealous, LBGTQ-adverse cellmate races to a room across campus.

It is six months following this "parting of the ways" when Robert receives the email. The email our daughter pleads with him not to share with me. *This* is then the moment when her *father* learns. *He* learns. That our "son" has always felt to be female, has known from the age of three or four that she *is* female. Despite her physicality her head tells her this. Just as naturally as her head works her math, her game strategy, her abstract thinking. Her head knows *this* too.

As requested by our "son," Robert alone lives with this

information for five agonizing days. Five days, before he makes an appointment with our psychologist to talk. In anguish, with desperation, with insurmountable pain, he goes to talk. But he had told me earlier that the news is "fine," "nothing bad." Referring then to the email that had been sent. The email we knew was coming, the email that would explain everything she mysteriously has been working on since starting school the previous fall. (S)he had made reference to these secret happenings with us for months by this time; the "mystery thing" about which she has long been occupied.

But all the while she has talked of this "work," she has declined to share any details with us. This was a secret. *The* secret. A secret between her new friends and her. She would explain all later. So it is this time later, through this email, that all is explained. To her father.

I will learn eventually the reason she is unwilling to reveal herself to me. The reason her former babysitter is told first off. Then her brother. Next her father. Our psychologist, he explains that it is the person from whom she fears rejection the most, *the* someone she cannot bear to suffer rejection, *the* person who is the most important person in her life, that is the person she cannot find the courage to tell.

And that is me.

Although, in addition, she is *mad* at me. Because of my looming, my *inevitable* rejection, she is mad. I, her mother, I do not deserve to know. It is, in fact, *none of my business*! As self-preservation, this is her excuse for not telling me. (S)he masks her fear of my rejection by holding desperately to her anger. She doesn't care if I go away! This is what she tells herself. This is what she tells her father. Over and over. Unconvincingly.

All the while this goes on, I endeavor to put this "*mystery thing*" from my mind. In its place, I work to convince myself that our years of despair are now over…all due to the mystery thing. Which is not bad.

As for Robert? He must tell me the truth as much for himself as from the advice our doctor has given him, has insisted upon. "In no uncertain terms," our doctor explains, "can you keep this from 'his' mother even a moment longer."

I am walking out the door when I get the call. It is early evening. Robert has asked me to stay around, he'll be home in twenty. But I have plans with friends and so I suggest we talk later. Then he tells me the conversation we will have is about the email, *the* email from Grant.

As known, I know simply one thing as concerns the email: It contains "nothing bad." So I tell him I will stay around but after our talk I will catch up with friends.

"No." He responds with "No."

So I am baffled, baffled because the news is "not bad." But now I am agitated. I know my heartache quota had long ago surpassed its limit. My anxiety then, all over again, is without restraint, as I wait for Robert to arrive.

We sit facing one another as he prepares to tell me. And this is when I see tears streaming down his face. Something that I had never witnessed before this time. Ever. And so I sink into a dark place. Incessantly there is a dark place for me. All the time deeper and all the time darker.

And next he tells me.

Then. Then I just sit. Stiffly. Upright. Hands folded. Eyes

facing forward, again focusing on the un-seeable. No tears. I am frozen. Just as the time I was told my young "son" would likely die due to hepatitis, I feel nothing. But this is not something I do calculatedly or do in any way purposeful. No. This freezing, this is involuntary. This too is self-preservation. I am now something other than flesh and blood; I do not, in any way, resemble something human. I am automatic. I am robotic. I will come to realize later, when I have the facility to self-restore, that to feel not a thing? This is the body's response to guard against feeling *everything.*

Robert suggests I call our "now daughter." Tell her I love her. That I will always love her. Constantly. Permanently I will love her.

And I will. So I call.

When I learn about her fear of my rejection, the wind is taken from me. How, ever, would a mother reject her child? *Ever?* But it happens. Too often this is what occurs. These are the mothers, the fathers, the siblings, that believe the act of changing physiques is an act of spite aimed personally at them. These are the people who believe it impossible to bear the inevitable judgement, the devastating rejection, which is certain to come their way from their community of friends, from extended family, from society as a whole. And so these people, they are frightened. And they are frightened correctly, because it will happen. They will not maintain relationships with all.

But to not overcome? This is weak. To not realize this is not an act aimed at them? This is ignorant. To not understand this person needs love, acceptance, and support more than *ever?* This is cruelty.

And to not recognize that changing physiques is a thing

infinitely more frightening than they are likely to ever experience? This is egocentric. This is blind. This is callous. This is spite.

And this is unimaginable.

But it was told to "Grant" over countless years, from her many doctors, each in turn, when they had advised "him" to prepare for rejection. Even from his mother.

But actually from me? "*This*" is for which she must prepare herself? Of *my* response? Of my refutation? This is something I cannot comprehend. *When? Ever!* have I not been unyieldingly frantic to "catch the ball"? The ball that has been tossed back and forth, back and forth, continuously out of range. That ball. *The ball that is farthest-reaching.* A ball that, for too long, I have been unable to grasp in order to prove, to reassure, that I will not drop it. With certainty, I will hold this ball all the tighter. And it will remain securely there, in my embrace, *always.*

forty-one

Moving Through the Stages of Grief

The day following my enlightenment, still when I am nothing but a mechanism lacking both sensation and thought, before what will soon become my ensuing rage, we take a trip north to visit our now-daughter. This is a Saturday. When we reach her dorm we call to let her know we're outside.

As we sit in the car, Robert takes a deep breath. He turns toward me and this is when I see his anguish, acute and crushing. Anguish. "I pray she's not wearing a dress. I'm not ready" is what he says. We both slip further into our seats, into our confusion.

Her nail polish is purple. She tells us her name is now Grace. These are the only changes. Otherwise it is still our "son" that stands before us. We take her to lunch. Her spirits are high. Her father, her brother, and now her mother have all accepted her. No one is going away. We reassure her over and over. We hug. She says she has started looking into hormone replacement therapy. This is when I ask if this is absolutely, without one doubt, the future she wants. Her answer? "It's either this or it's suicide."

I don't ask again.

By this time she has contacted and gone to see two doctors in her university town of Bellingham, Washington. This is a relatively small town situated two hours north of Seattle. A town where both doctors, one after the other, are unapologetic as they refuse to assist her. There is no effort to conceal their distaste. Judgement is severe. I advise her not to contact any additional doctors in this town. I'll look into the matter when back home.

And this is when I find a doctor who has honed her work, dedicated her practice, to transgender health. These individuals are all this woman sees. She is twenty years experienced in her elected practice. She is respected and, appreciatively, she is respectful. She is both approachable and patient. And so this is where my daughter goes. And this is where, and this is when, she is properly educated about, and is courteously provided, hormone replacement therapy.

As for me? It is now, during my robotic phase, I begin to read book after book, eventually going through a large abundance of them. The subject is gender identity. What does it mean to be transgender? I learn entirely new concepts; I learn an entire new vocabulary. I learn I have been naïve as to an entirely alternative way of being.

Having never before considered, never contemplated certain distinctions, I now understand the clear division between gender identity and sexual orientation. Between transgender and cisgender. Between gender fluid and having a concrete knowledge of yourself as either male or as female. And this concrete knowledge, this is true, despite whether one's body and brain are in agreement on the subject, or if they are incompatible. I learn it is the brain that decides whether a person is gay, lesbian, bisexual, heterosexual, transgender, cisgender, or gender fluid. The brain decides this, not the body.

I learn there is a large gap between crossdresser and transgender. One being identified by the reversal of the type of clothes typically worn by the opposite sex. The other, more serious other, is the sex mismatch between body and brain.

I compile all this knowledge, this note taking, and I create a folder. And I make a handful of copies. When done, a month later, I will distribute these folders, filled with newfound awareness, to extended family.

But, at present, my now-daughter has forbidden me from telling anyone about her true identity, least of all the rest of our family: grandparents, aunts, uncles, our special cousin. She fears rejection. Robert, he is back hard at work. His talking about this turbulent news; this is not desired. In all honesty, this is not slightly, not remotely, a conversation he wants to have.

But I cannot bear it. I need someone to talk with. Desperately I need my sister. This is also a time I refuse to see my psychologist. What's the point? After twenty-four years my son is now my daughter. And my daughter? She is six-feet, five inches tall. She is the tallest person in our family, extended and otherwise. Her brother is six-feet-two and her father is five-feet-ten. And I am complete with guilt, repeatedly the guilt. And this guilt is because I look female and she does not.

Moreover, everyone we have ever known, have ever met, knows I have two sons. Former teachers, friends, current and past. Neighbors, our family doctor, our dentist, our pharmacist. The list moves forward, the list goes on and on. And I must tell each and every one. The job is daunting. Terrifying. And unbearable. Because this will be the time I will begin to feel *everything*.

Three weeks pass before I tell my sister. Despite that I have not yet been granted permission, I talk with my sister. Because I am desperate. Because I need this. And this is the moment I begin to feel *all*, *everything*, the moment grief, loss, terror, and hopelessness invade, and spread throughout.

But, before this, before the time the flood will settle, prior to the month when I will leave the house never, when I will rise from my bed very little, the time before I will feel *everything*, there is another phase it seems I must pass through. And this phase? This is the time I embrace a rage I never knew would have existed within me. And I will hold to this phase, this fury, tightly because if I do not grab hold of something I will sink into the pain that will take hold of all of me. The pain that will then force me downward, hold me under and drown.

And the focus of my rage? This is my brother Steven. And the reason? The reason I convince myself, assure myself that *I hate him! I hate him! I hate him!*

This is for his belief that gay life is an aberrant, deviant life. And this is due to my further assumption that he feels transgender is likewise a scam, malformed and improper. A body and brain mismatch that doesn't truly exist, *could* never exist. Would and *should* never exist. Transgender, this is an impossibility, a claim for which the world is not prepared to tolerate, an assertion for which the world should never have to tolerate. The simple truth: Transgender is an excuse to live an errant life.

This is what I allow myself to believe of him. This is what I allow to pervade within so as to nourish and build my rage.

And with all my "*certainty*," due to my "*knowing*" of his inflexibility and bold convictions and owing to the abundance of pain this creates in my child's world and in my world, the misery this advances throughout the world, *I Hate Him*!

And too, I know he has never lived with a brain other than his own. He has never been told by his brain that he is anything other than a heterosexual, cisgender man. He has never had this occur. And so I am rooted in my assertion. I am rooted in "*his assertion*"; "*I know, without doubt*" he holds that others' heads are offering up the same information as his. "*This is what I am certain of.*"

And. I. Hate. Him.

But all this rage, I keep it within and I guard it there closely so that it creates nothing but destruction and turmoil inside my spinning head and hostility inside my cold heart. And then it comes soon enough, with all this inward tumult that I become physically ill. My rage and my hatred, it does this. I buckle over with this rage that is emotional and physical. And revengeful.

Haven't I been through enough without *this*? Without my brother and *his insights*, *his convictions*, which have now come to close? Haven't I been through enough without the burden of my loathing? Haven't I had an ample amount of "bucking up"? But never mind, I will carry on with the storm I have created within, the rage that permeates. Because…

I hate him!

I hate him!

I hate him!

And this is what I tell myself, and this is what I continue feeding myself, for three exhausting weeks. Until I allow myself the truth, the truth I've known all along, because my brother, he does love my child, *this* is what I am certain of. And *this* is what is true despite my need to think otherwise. He wishes for her to be well. He wishes for me to be well.

And so my rage abates as I remember this. And too he doesn't judge, not in the least. He accepts the truth of transgender. His mind has long since changed regarding gays.

Therefore I am proven wrong. And this is when it comes that I can no longer hold my anger up as a shield. It is simply too heavy. I am simply too exhausted. And then, as feared, it is as soon as I let rage go, that I begin to feel *everything*.

And this is the time I take to my bed for a month. I simply lie there, at once limp and lifeless, agitated and terrified. Engulfed by my memories and my terrors. Drowning from the pain of them.

And despite the books I've read, although the knowledge I've acquired through those books: The fact that trans people, particularly those with family support, can go on to live normal lives, some become surgeons, maybe lawyers, teachers or chefs, people who assimilate into the larger population. Individuals who have people who love and admire them. People who marry. But, even so, I am powerless to calm myself. Instead my fears trigger what I also know, and I see the murders that occur, as transgender people, even those who have successfully assimilated, are subjected to the highest percentage of victimization above any other peoples. By many fold. I see suicide, as the rate of suicide within the transgender community exceeds that of any other group. By margins. I see poverty and homelessness all based on discrimination, harassment, assault and the ignorance of others. I see drug addiction and early death by overdose. I envision a shortened life on the outskirts. A lonely life. A life of misery.

I succumb entirely to my fears and I don't know how to go on. I move in and out of sleep. I exhaust myself with tears.

And I recall something Grace had said to our former sitter months ago. But this woman, she is loyal to my child, she is loyal to both my children, genuinely loyal, and rightfully so, therefore she had agreed to the silence which Grace had desperately needed for their future bond, for the trust that bond would require. But after Grace's outing she tells Robert a detail. A detail that overcomes. Because Grace had said this: "My transformation, this is not something I am doing just to be invited back to the ornament party."

When I learn of this I understand I am hearing the words of "his" four-year-old self. An innocence left behind decades ago.

And this crushes. Profoundly it conquers another part of me. The memory of "him" as him, the memory of "him" before all our years of despair, this I cannot bear. But I am now confronted, *defeated* by the image of that day, the day he won the coveted Santa star.

"It will be a memory to grasp ever-firmly and hold passionately close, because this star marks for me a day when the universe decided to play fair with my child."

My memories, these are the everything I wish to silence.

forty-two

The Cruelty
in Ignorance

This was a quiet, warm day back when Grant was in high school. I am driving. My windows rolled down in order to welcome in the air, the warmth of it. I have been with my most recent psychologist. Another of my own endless appointments with doctors. My emotional health is not good, habitually not good. In every way I am a mess. Always a mess. This is another time, a time within forever times, I don't care whether I live or whether I die.

As a result I am somber. I have been crying. A lot. And as I have cried myself into exhaustion, as I am now depleted of any and of all foreseeable tears, my face has become passive. Suspended. Unresponsive. Do I look angry? Haughty? Arrogant? I don't know.

I am a culmination of inside clutter and numbness. Both at once. A frozen, expressionless, exhausted mess.

I approach a light just after it switches to red and I stop behind the waiting car in front of me. Unfocused on my surroundings I do this. Unaware of other cars, other drivers.

A man pulls forward in the lane next to my own. He drives a

tall truck, windows also rolled down as far as is possible. Slowly he coasts until adjacent to where I sit waiting. He brakes then, and despite there is room to move forward he doesn't. It seems, instead, he has come to this precise spot, makes to rest at this exact location, purposefully.

He turns toward me next and begins to speak over the idling traffic. He says, "Hey! You!" his voice is forceful, harsh. It is in this manner that he wants my attention.

I turn and I glance over, my expression passive. But his look communicates…revulsion? Loathing? When he speaks again he says, "If you had a white streak you'd look just like Cruella De Vil." Then, having passed judgment, his face shows satisfaction. He gins darkly. Smugly.

The light changes and he's gone. I make it half a block before I am able to pull to the side of the road. Once parked I find I do have tears available, new tears. Always more tears. I lean over, forehead pressed against the steering wheel, and I cry. An hour passes before I am able to bring myself to leave and drive forward anew.

Sometime during the course of that same year I learn of a woman, to be exact, I learn of a woman I know, have known since the age of five, who holds week-long writing classes for struggling teens. This as a means to express any deep anguish or to understand any trauma that may be at the root of their suffering. With this knowledge these young adults will then be able to confront their problems "head on," and by way of this overcome any distress attached to them.

This is what can happen. This is what this woman has witnessed over and over in this ideal, "everyone deserves a break" world. Again and again.

And so I ask Grant, "Will you please participate?"

He will, he tells me, "I guess," sluggishly uttered.

Although despite his indifference, I am relieved, surprised but relieved.

We're inside the entry of her early twentieth century home, this woman and me. This is one day before I will introduce her to Grant. She is before me as we speak. Both of us standing. Her clothes, her manner, these give off an unassuming aspect. Simplistically so. Her hands are expressive. Gentle movement. She used to be a ballerina, her graceful ways a part of her still. Her straight black hair, pretty, but allowed to turn gray. A cut nondescript. Her clothes non-form fitting, but comfortable. Oversized, despite her thin frame.

Style? The bother of it? It seems these are affairs with which she does not concern herself. She involves herself rather with important matters in life. Hard realities. Truth.

The saving of children.

Accordingly she is everything that is attentive and reliably earnest. As her caring words and soft voice express.

Can it be she possesses a selflessness the extent of which is unreachable by any other? A moral purity unknown to yet one more?

She is the older sister of a childhood friend. Two years my senior. *Lightyears* my senior. Or so it seems. I have never known her well. But what I do remember is that she "knows" herself, she *understands herself at the deepest level.* And she conveys this through the passing on of sage advice, and she suggests this with chosen words that at all times carry weight. And, as for others? It seems she understands others better than they understand themselves. *She understands me.*

Consequently, she has the expertise to fix anyone.

She has the expertise to fix my son.

And she has the expertise to fix me all in the course.

"I'm glad you're here," she starts. "I believe Grant will feel better once he's completed his work." Spoken with a concerned, even touching, personal involvement with me.

I pause then. I take a deep breath. And next I begin to describe my son; I lay bare our situation. To a woman I have known my entire life. A woman who is thoughtful, openly empathetic, a woman I trust…

And I say this: "Grant hides from life, hides away from himself. He sleeps." I continue: "He doesn't go out, he doesn't socialize. Even during the time he had not sequestered himself he had socialized very little. And he never talks with girls, has never had a girlfriend." I expose myself further: "He suffers," I tell her. "And alongside him, I suffer too."

And *this* is when the blow comes. The knock-the-wind from me, throw-me-to-the-ground no-longer-steeped-in-moral-purity-nor-immersed-in-selfless-virtue, blow.

Quietly she looks at me. Silently she assesses me. This is what she does before she speaks. "Why would he need a girlfriend when he already has one in you?" she asks in judgement.

And before I am able to fully digest her words, she continues to impart further "wisdom" on me, to me.

"You're not suffering, not truly." She says this next.

She had a daughter who had wanted to take her life; this is how she knows.

"This is suffering. Your child is alive. Be grateful you're not actually suffering." And this is the manner in which she enlightens me as to how I feel.

Or rather, *how I do not feel.*

And *this* is the moment I am jolted awake.

Okay…

Whoa.

Stop! the stampede… I have come across another "expert" in my long string of "experts" who thinks she understands my world? Understands my son? Understands that he is literally dying? Has considered that his father and I agonize every waking hour that he may take his life at any moment? Has taken steps to know his desperation? Has asked about his tears and has experienced him when he is frantic for an embrace? Has inquired about the angst in his voice when pleading for my reassurance, my acceptance, and my love?

Has taken the time to yet meet Grant before laying down her verdict? Before delivering her mistreatment?

Another "expert"?

Whoa.

Despite my anger, I work to distance myself from this woman's words, from her language. Language that is everything sugar and swirl. Words that are all things serrated and bitter.

Rather I concentrate on my son. I encourage him to write.

Which he does.

Some.

Before retreating to his room.

Another time over.

Then… it is two months since learning my son is my daughter, two frozen turned enraged, turned "everything" months, this is when all *this* cruelty occurs…

It is a holiday weekend but none of this business of festivities registers within. I have forgotten about our city-wide celebration that will begin the following day. My plans for the weekend? I will be inside attending a conference on gender diversity. I will take classes and I will participate in discussion groups.

And I'm sacred to be there. I am afraid I will cry, make a scene. I am afraid of what I will learn, or what I won't understand. I am afraid.

Robert does not join me in doing this. It is overwhelming. It is, in fact, impossible to understand what's happened. It is unbearable to accept that his son is no longer his son. He needs more time.

But graciously it is my sister who does come to my side. Saves me. Joins me. Directs me. Holds my hand. Because, as time has elapsed my sister and I have grown wiser, closer. Mindful of our past. No longer am I separated out. And my sister, she joins me because, in all honesty, I am lucky enough to have the best sister in the world.

But before this conference will begin, one day earlier, I am at the grocery. This I do as if I know to stock up on chips and dip, soda and beer. I'm there, alongside the hordes of others who do intend to supply up for the weekend's events.

I have placed my many items on the moving belt and I stand prepared to swipe my card. But again, and again unknowingly, I have made someone angry. This, once more, likely due to my dream-like gaze which wanders off and away. An unregistered disregard as to my surroundings.

"You can see I'm working alone." This is the clerk who berates me. "Pretty obvious I have no one to bag groceries. Pretty obvious there's a long line of people behind you." He says all this with intensity. With the intensity of his rage. "I guess you're not too happy to be here. I guess you just don't care about anyone but yourself."

And then I wake up.

And next I leave the store. Without purchasing a thing, I leave. I do this for all his cruel ignorance. And in doing so I burden him with all the additional work of un-bagging the items he had just bagged. The burden of voiding and explaining away my would-have-been purchases. The problem of the groceries going nowhere without him expending time and effort. The burden of appeasing his ever-increasing, long stretch of impatient shoppers.

And I leave him with the burden of his rage.

I just leave.

forty-three

A Job

Grace needs, and too, Grace desperately wants to be surrounded by others. Therefore she finds an apartment in her college town with a couple who have placed an ad. This after a long, lonely summer spent in a house beside a lake relatively near campus. A *"would be happy"* place, if one were happy...

She and I together, we tackle the logistics of the move. Heavy, bulky items: her mattress, her desk, dresser, kitchen items and the like are taken from the lake house down and around two interior flights of stairs, followed by two exterior flights, one short, one longer, and stuffed into the back of my car. Having arrived at her new quarters, these items are then hauled across a parking lot, down another flight of stairs, where we now encounter a longer flight heading back up, which leads to and across a narrow hallway and then inside the apartment door. We pass through the interior hallway, shorter this time, and maneuver these pieces sideways or angled fittingly around the door and, at long last, inside her tiny room. Subsequently we drive back to the lake house where we again gather up, box up, and carry items off to my car. We cart all these additional articles to her new apartment and set them inside. Before done we must repeat this hauling three times.

But she's in.

During her interval there the three roommates become friends. Although the other two, they are a committed couple, and so most often they are off by themselves. And therefore, once again, too often Grace is alone.

In addition she is not enrolled in school. She has made the decision to delay until winter quarter. She must prepare. Emotionally she must do this. She must ready herself, all over, to place herself among countless people. She is lonely when alone. She is lonely in a crowd. What she needs, that what she desires, is intimacy. One person or a number that is small, that is what works best.

But too, owing to her delay there is no structure to her days. No purpose to leave the house but for food. Others from high school, those who had also enrolled in this same college, a handful who were friends, had graduated at minimum three years prior. Every one of them has moved on. Additional friends she had made in earlier years have full-time jobs or are in graduate school away. Some are now married and live elsewhere. Others, those currently in school, are in healthier, brighter places. They live bolder lives. And too they are younger, some by up to five years. Although, by all means practical, these younger students are older. Advanced in emotional maturity. In greater world experience. They live well beyond her too-often-confined life, and her present-day fifteen years.

And, all over, I am frightened to put too many demands on her. Moreover I feel the "game," the requirements to put down, have changed now that we understand she is ever more fragile than I can bear.

Nevertheless, once more, our psychologist insists we get firm again. She will find a job. More to get out of her apartment than to earn money. Immediately, however, she resists this condition, so "tough love" reveals its devastating head once more. Again we back her into a tight corner. In order to receive money for rent, for food, she must get out. She must find employment. She cannot return home. These are the binding rules.

I want to embrace her. I want her away. Forever my state is emotional disarray. But then, that which is true, truly the best, is that she doesn't wish to return home. And she needs this apartment, this shelter. She needs the money we provide. In the end she has no choice but to comply.

And this is when she finds a job washing dishes at a restaurant relatively close by. Still, this restaurant is far enough that a bus must be taken. Okay…bus. Job. People. Outer world.

Progress.

But yet there is a catch. Persistently another challenge. Because as now understood, she is passionate for companionship. True friendship. Not the dizzying crowd companionship of co-employees while busy at work.

However, these are the people she has close at hand. And these people are those who make up the greater population, the masses. Those who have never put their lives on hold or evaded the countless others who make up community. They are the people who have lived through numerous and inescapable interactions that provide a natural and progressive understanding of the social world. These people make up the majority, the mainstream, the bulk. They are those who, by no effort of their own, rest securely inside one of the two center slots of normal distribution.

It happens then that she tries too vigorously, too desperately, in her attempt to re-enter the world. Anxiously she wants to be like "everyone else," to exist like "everyone else." To settle without difficulty into the majority.

And then too, added to every bit of this conundrum, is hormone therapy. Her desperation for people is wildly, heartlessly escalated by the female hormones she now takes. Her entire being is distorted. Cruelly so. She cries unpredictably. She cries uncontrollably for hours. And she wishes for someone to rescue her from her misery. She feels hollow. She cannot find the person who lives within, cannot access even a small portion of herself that can stand on her own. She needs someone, anyone, to stand with her. To stand for her. To save her.

It comes next, that within a few months, she leaves this job. Is "let go" from this job. She needs to get herself "together." Her coworkers? They cannot save her. Her manager speaks with her. And this is when I instruct her to call me whenever desperation takes control. And so I receive phone call after phone call. Many at 1:00, 2:00, and 3:00 in the morning. She cries and I listen. I make suggestions. I make uncountable trips north. We talk. She cries. We hug. I cry as I drive home.

All during this time, and ever since her days at the lake house, she has been talking with an off-campus psychologist. And, once she concedes to herself, to me, that she has broken down another time, once she admits she cannot, on her own, raise herself, this is when she asks me again to come north. She would like me to join in a session.

We meet outside the office of her new doctor, a woman I have not met. I am introduced and welcomed. I sit on one end of the sofa the doctor has situated to face the chair where she herself sits. Grace stretches across the length of this sofa, her head in my lap. Her long legs extend beyond, well beyond, the arm at the opposite end.

The doctor says very little during our session. Mostly she listens as I speak to Grace who then responds occasionally. I stroke her head. She relaxes. The doctor adds a few comments. When we leave she thanks me in private. She herself had been uncertain of what to do next apart from asking family to get involved.

After our session I bring my broken daughter home.

Where she will remain another year more.

forty-four

Learning Curve

During this current interval, this third hiatus at home, we attend a birthday party at the home of "Grant's" "second family." This again is her closest friend Brandon, and this is six weeks since her announcement. Included among the crowd are parents, siblings, cousins, additional friends. And too, grandparents are present. Grandparents beyond eighty, who, in all likelihood, will be unable to comprehend that their grandson's best friend, a "boy" they've known over fifteen years, is now female. At this point she doesn't appear female. They have not been enlightened as to any transformation on the horizon.

There comes a time in the evening when I sit next to the grandmother. During our talk she asks about "Grant."

"How is he doing?" she asks. "What is he up to?" she inquires. "He's such a nice boy," she adds.

At this moment I feel it impossible, pointless even, to correct her use of pronouns. Attempting an explanation? I believe this would be an endless, *exhausting*, task. And then too, our talk is likely to conclude without understanding. And there is *this*, always *this*: I fear my now-daughter will experience ever-more rejection.

And so, as I respond to this woman's inquiries, I mimic her use of pronouns. I mimic the *wrong* pronouns. And regretfully I do this as Grace passes close behind and overhears. But her passing close, her overhearing, this is something of which I am unaware.

Once having ended our conversation I get up to move around the room. Soon enough I notice Grace is not anywhere I can see. She's not in the living room, nor is she in the kitchen. She is not in the dining room. I wait fifteen minutes before beginning my search. Then I find her. She has retreated to a back room where she sits alone. When I enter she looks up, and with eyes that express all the pain she feels she says to me, "I'm not a *he*."

I am silent for a moment. Dread fills. I find I am unable, or unwilling, to explain the reason for what I've done. I understand I have been tactless, insensitive. I've made the wrong choice, a hurtful choice. I apologize to her. But what she says next baffles. Thoroughly this complicates all this pronoun difficulty yet further, because, she informs me then that, in addition to "she," "her," and "hers," it is acceptable to refer to her as "they," "them," and "theirs."

These pronouns, which since always have indicated more than one person, the plural? These are now suitable in reference to an individual as well.

Pronouns…they are my newfound enemy.

Still, there is another forbidding adversary that overwhelms. Bathrooms.

Public restrooms…and the use of them.

This is something the greater population may not understand… the pain, the excruciating heartache felt by a person who is obliged to use a bathroom of the gender they are not…the *wrong* bathroom. A room which they have, for many agonizing years, been required to enter and to use. A room where no one within their surroundings will realize the person they sincerely are. This wrong room, this is where they feel fenced-in among people who, in all ways genuine, are nothing like themselves.

And too…in using a bathroom which honors their truthful selves? This is dangerous.

On one side lives anguish, a profound pain for which these individuals have always suffered, heartbreaking agony added to the many (way too many) obstacles that confront and challenge. Obstacles for which numerous have, and will continue, to take their lives.

On the other side exists danger. And this danger, this is emotional, this is verbal and this is physical. Sometimes the risk of entering a restroom that recognizes the truth of themselves can be life-threatening. This is especially true when an individual who is female is yet unrecognizable as such. This is especially true when this person is very tall. Both of which are the case with my daughter.

And alongside her I am frightened.

She agrees one evening, while still at home, to join Robert and me in seeing a movie. At a theater. Out *there*. In a theater where public restrooms exist. And, as follows, when the movie ends, this is the time we both have need of a restroom.

She follows me in. But until we are inside, I am unaware of this coming in behind. And when I do become aware, I want to shrivel…I want her away… And for this sentiment, shame on me.

But she cannot survive, yet one time more, using the incorrect bathroom. This simply brings about too much misery. Too much falling apart. Too many memories of falling apart.

Until you are in another person's skin…

Although, along with wanting *her* out of the women's room, I want *myself* away. Again I wish to dissolve, become invisible.

Shame, then. Shame. Shame. My immeasurable shame.

And this women's room? This is large. And this women's room? This is largely occupied. Very young, young, old, older yet. These are the occupants. Who scowl. Who openly reveal loathing. Some who appear fearful.

And, as a result, all this brings on further emotional distress. For us both.

But as for verbal abuse, this doesn't happen. Not this time.

As for the man waiting outside ready to receive news of the "intruder"? The "pervert"? He's not there.

Not this time...

Despite dodging the unthinkable, I again cannot access air. I am dizzy from the air I cannot access. But when the three of us make our way to the exit, as we stand on the sidewalk outdoors, I discover, once again, there is a tiny amount of oxygen to take in.

So gently I take some in.

My endless burden to toughen up, to advance my awareness... this is a weight I must accept, swallow and accept. Period. And too I'm tired of all this "toughening," this "advancing," which only progresses toward the difficult and the confusing. At times toward the near impossible.

And the everything...

But advancing I must.

And I will, slowly, painfully. Eventually. Yet, the instant she informed her name was now Grace I sank. How would I do this? Refer to her by a name other than Grant? The name we had carefully chosen for "him" at birth.

This overwhelms. And too, this is loaded with pitfalls as dangerous as pronouns.

But, once more, I must step up.

I am now obliged to send emails to a new account, one she has set up to represent her correct name. *Her* chosen name. Her soon-to-be-legal name. I must adjust her name in my phone list. I will instruct others to do so as well. Her birth certificate will need updating so as to depict her accurate name as well as her correct gender. Her identification card, in addition, will need this. Her university card, her passport too. At the pharmacy she insists on the name that represents her truthful self. The insurance company will need to be informed. And too, she wants this process begun without delay. I will help her do this. Even before I've had adequate time to process the shift. Even before I've had adequate time to raise myself from the anguish of the shift.

The shift…

Buck up, Sandra…

But as if never enough, there is another obstacle I must gather the courage to rise above, or not. Family photos. Childhood photos of her as him. These are painful, believe excruciating to look at. Simply glancing their way can, all over again, bring about the *everything*.

The impossible *everything*.

These are the photos of her childhood self; they are the photos of my two "sons" where they occupy the same frame. And many of these memories, they sit on my dresser. There is the large portrait that hangs on the wall upstairs; the two matching painted portraits, one of each "son" displayed on the upper floor as well.

They are the photos taken at birth, throughout toddlerhood and all the active years going forward. They are records of young faces peering down from our ceiling hole. All those years of Fourth of July bake sales. Playing at the lake or digging in the sand on the saltwater beach in front of their grandparents' home. Of visiting the mountains. Of visiting Santa. First days of school, firsts in general. Et cetera and et cetera, and memory et cetera.

These photos…

They are the photos that mark a time our family was whole… *lucky*. The years before all fell apart. The times when my children were best friends. Those fleeting and busy years our family was happy.

I can't bear to look at these photos.

Desperately I need these photos.

Immensely I want these photos.

These photos of a family that once was…

But Grace, she wants all these taken down. Off and away. Tossed. She cannot suffer the images of those years as she hid the truth from herself, as she hid the truth from us. She cannot endure all those years of looking at the person she is not. A person she has never been.

So once more I do the undoable. For her. I box them up, and I bury them away. I do this, as if our past had never existed. As if our former life had never mattered.

My learning curve? This, instead, is a vertical line, sheer and painfully ever-rising.

forty-five

Never

After the talk with Grace's psychologist, her newest doctor up north, we discover her meds must be increased. By a lot. This in order to battle against the destabilizing hormones she takes.

Moreover, although aware of her heightened instability, and while fully mindful of her most recent breakdown, our doctor tells us, once again, that she cannot pause. Still she cannot carry on living at home while hiding away. "Regardless of escalating fear, amid unstable emotions," he says, "she must get out."

And this is when I fully realize the "game," this horrendous, impossible, frightening "game" will never change.

As in times before, every piece of me is thrown into panic, and, as such, I labor excessively to keep this directive at bay... for as long as possible.

And I manage to do this, to avoid my doctor with his terrifying advice, for three months. Up until his persistent and ever-amplifying urging shakes me back to reality. To the impossible reality of our lives. Therefore, this becomes another time we instruct Grace to leave the house for eight hours every day.

It is during this interval that she takes a writing class at a nearby community college. This school is situated within a notably diverse part of town, and too, this school, in itself, is notably diverse. As follows the faculty, the students, they are readily (and notably) accepting of all.

Early on while attending this class, she puts down on paper the struggles she has lived through, is living through, by way of being transgender.

As the assignment comes to completion, the students are required to pass their papers around for comment, before they will be handed back to their author.

The comments my daughter then receives? These include: *"Grow a pair."* *"What the hell?"* *"Man-up!"*

The abuse, the judgement, this is endless. Will always be endless. Even among a "notably diverse accepting" crowd.

forty-six

A Family in Fragments

Parker is now two months into further study, eight weeks into this school that follows when, shouldering his "responsibility" for success, weighed down by his "duty" to be the one child that comes through, carrying his never-to-end quest to be noticed, embraced, by his parents, he escapes. To Mexico.

And this disappearance comes once he has shut down his email, turned off his phone. Directly after he has put on hold any Facebook access. This is the time he vanishes.

Unaware of his flight, I don't know to check in with him until a week has passed. But it is a day following this week when I do call. And it is atypical when I don't reach him. I attempt next to make contact for the following three days. Three days of calls, turned emails, followed by texts, with no response. This is then the time I phone his school. The registrar, she had spoken with Parker about his future academic plans. This was eight days prior. Since that time they have not been in contact.

He is unresponsive. He is no longer in contact with his school. Literally he has gone missing...and I wilt. In addition, I have not been informed of any changes in academic plans. Neither, what is certain, has Robert. The registrar is forbidden to say a word as concerns this.

And too, why? This baffles. Thoroughly this confuses. The California Institute of Technology, a school at which to achieve acceptance is a near-impossible feat? This school, that had selected him for a PhD program as simply one of three students world-wide to whom they would offer a position? This school, which covers full exorbitant tuition, and has granted him thousands of additional dollars for outside expenses? A program which is bestowed millions in research, prized resources, and extensive travel paid by interested entities…an education where notable contacts and assured employment will be immediately and bound-lessly secured… Why alter this after two short months? Why do so, ever?

Immediately I phone one of his two closest friends. But this boy, he has been sworn into secrecy. About Parker's disappearance. As concerns his whereabouts. Nevertheless, it is at this moment that this cherished friend, this companion who is deeply loved by our entire family, has become my formidable opponent. There will be no not informing me of my son's location, of his deser-tion. This, I make known, is indisputable.

And that is the moment I learn he is in Mexico. He had gone there to think. And he had gone there in order to climb its high-est peak. And he had gone there…alone.

I shrink further from this information, emotionally and phys-ically I do this. But it is next when this friend offers a fragment of news, albeit a critical piece of information, that temporarily saves me: Parker is down. He had climbed this mountain, but now he is down. In addition he had met two other climbers before his ascent and the three had summited together. They had roped-up in a line of safety. They had watched out for one another. And he is down.

Despite this vital news I yet work to stay afloat. While my head spins, even though my body falters, I attempt this. Then, it is a moment later when I learn his phone is back on. And so I call.

And he picks up. Mercifully, he picks up.

He will call his father and me in three days' time, the time he will be back in the US. He will tell us all then, about his departure, about his academic future. The inattention he has suffered. His anger. His hurt. The too-many years of laboring to survive it all.

And so we wait.

My children as children, is this what I want? Of course not. Not truly. And too, this is what I cannot have. But to guard them, envelop them in my protection, for that reason, why not desire to move back to a time when Parker too received my devoted focus, my dedicated attention? And how have I never been able to see that he is, in fact, not fine as I had always perceived, had always believed? *Had always needed to believe…* Why not wish for the years when my two young "sons" were best friends? Back when Parker was happy? Back when "Grant" was happy? How has our family become so lost, so impossibly difficult to save? How did it all become so very, very frightening?

When one is broken, all are broken…

And it refuses to let up, broken.

Rather we are presented with circumstance followed by unforgiving circumstance that precludes us from mending the damage.

Therefore at present, and although Robert and I have become

aware of Parker's suffering, *the degree of his suffering*, he, *even now*, will not be our sole focus. He, even now *cannot* be our sole focus. And this is because, aside from his flight, his profound hurt, this is also the time we send Grace away. Tell her to leave… instruct her to find a shelter. For the homeless. *This* is what we demand of *our child*.

Unimaginably, *this* is what we require, what we heartlessly *insist* of our shattered daughter. And this decision, this decree of which the memory continues to crush each of us? This again is owing to our cognitive psychologist and his firm advice, his insistent pressing. This sending her off, he had said, is our last resort. Our ultimate recourse. This again is tough love.

We must do this for her.

And so we do the undoable. Unbearably we send her away. *This* is what we must do *for her*. *This* is what *I* must do. *For her*. Along with her father, I too do the unthinkable. In order for her to heal…or fall again…I am required to condemn my own child off and away and adrift. My once upon a time, two pound, nine-and-a-half-ounce preemie, bipolar, transgender, pan-phobic, enormously sensitive child, again, and as always, fighting for her life, I must abandon her to passing her days wandering the streets, and spending her afternoons searching for shelter… or not…and only if there is room at the inn.

forty-seven

A *Mother* in Fragments

The result of our unending crises, my pain and countless years of confusion and fear… Well, this is the time I come apart for real. My two children, both directionless. Both hurting. And I am entirely without means to save them. Entirely without a way to momentarily hold them. Hold on to them. Unbearably I am without any way to say I'm sorry.

And too my falling apart? Heartlessly this assaults without moderation as it overpowers *any and all* reason I may have earlier possessed. Is that the way of all breakdowns? Is it that *every aspect* of coming apart, *each detail* of slipping away, must be madness?

Days emerge then when I become ridiculous, irrefutably absurd. Far, far out of balance. Completely, it seems, without means to keep myself in check. I transform into a genuine bonafide kook. I do this as if I have been taken prisoner, captured by some mind-altering drug. And this transformation, this occurs at times fully unanticipated. Mercilessly, without warning, this drug invades and establishes its dominion only to show me that everything is "hilarious," that *I* am hilarious. Or as sidesplitting as one would imagine an adult, fully-grown, to be when ludicrous. Silly. Foolish. Trivial. Juvenile.

I am everything that is madness and yes, robotic. Both at once. And this is the manner in which the transformation of me gets underway.

-●

Parallel play

Similar to the time in one's life when socialization is engaged in a process of parallel play, I am now markedly similar to those two-and-three-year-olds who play side by side, all the while unaware of another in their surrounds. Yes, I too no longer have regard for those nearby. Other adults, all of whom remain adults during my idiocy, for me they are simply not present. It is, in fact, impossible for them to exist in my private, senseless world. My childlike world of parallel play.

We are out to dinner and I am *so very comical*. And it is *just that*…my "comical," my unchecked and very funny self, all due to a disconnect from my reality entirely too painful, that allows me a night out. My emotions, my mind, these are both turned off, controlled rather by an influence unknowable. Incomprehensible. Imperceptible.

There are four of us. Another couple, Robert and me. We are sharing wine. And we are consuming a fair amount of it. The restaurant, this is not white tablecloth, but too, it is not altogether without sophistication. The lights are moody, discerningly turned low. There are courses…appetizers to share, salads, maybe soup. There are main dishes followed by dessert. "Let's skip coffee." Always more wine.

We overindulge.

I overindulge.

And this is when Ms. Gladys Knight herself enters the room. Yes, I begin to sing. In the restaurant. Which is full. Which is filled with diners who would undoubtedly like to be at peace and not otherwise subjected to my song… her song. A song that surely she wrote with me in mind, the lyrics so personal. Words longing a return to a simpler time, a simpler place, if just for a moment. And I repeat these lyrics she wrote for me. Over and over. And I grow louder and louder as I do so.

So, so, very, very funny…

The waitress scowls. Other diners, if strolling past, they stare. They gaze over at the scene of it, of me.

I've embarrassed our friends, Robert.

I giggle.

Although once home, when alone, I cry…the hilarious robot, she cries. She sheds tears as the metal and bolts of her once-again attempt to pull apart in order to bring forth a human. This is what the robot does, as she fights to remain in one walled-in piece.

What is the word, a sufficient word, to describe the indignity of those memories? And others equal to them? The handful of other days, evenings, where again I embrace a world where only I exist? Where only children belong? A world where I alone play silly?

Humiliation—no, not strong enough, not exact enough. Mortification…mortification and disgrace…both words combined come closer.

And without question that day will arrive, the day mortification and disgrace will force introspection. Render me silent, motionless. And ashamed.

Although, before that day, I, all over again, must pass through another stage…one more troubling, *exhausting stage*. Just for me.

Therefore, in concert with my "hilarious," in combination with my steely armor, this double personality? Is that anger circles back to wound another time.

And I am so very, very weary of anger…

Moreover, the focus of my fury *this time around*? Is Robert. *He* is now the object of all the wrath that plagues me. In addition, I have come to realize that I have been for years overextended angry at him. I am incensed over his too many elongated intervals as he's checked out. I fume over his not sharing fairly the load of the devastation, the emotional ruin, which primarily I alone have carried. And I burn over his burying himself in work. And now I awaken to this…again.

To anger.

Who was I twenty years ago? Those years before my oldest stopped living "his" life? Before we condemned her to the streets? Those years in advance of my youngest falling invisible? In advance of him falling off the grid? Who was I before all the anger? Will I recover a trace of the person I used to be? At this moment I can't see a path to recovery. At this moment I have lost all thread of my former self.

And what became of my long-ago mothering plans? That foolproof course set in place in order to assure the sort of mother I would someday be? I consider then the bold moment I had lain down, in all cast-iron certainty, my mothering future…

What became of that?

Well the future, it seems, has plans of its own.

While promises…even those made with yourself? They too find a way of falling to pieces…

forty-eight

Escape

And I flee... I simply escape the heartache I know will someday be necessary to stand before, heartache to confront and to defeat. And I run because reliving all this? Feeling all that, for too many years, has transpired? Suffering all this present rage? The pain over my children? My infinite anxiety? The failure of my starry-eyed plans? This is undoable. This is impossible.

So just go!

And that is what I do.

I settle then into our much-loved mountain town. I go there because I am familiar with it. Because I feel safe there. Because it seems I refuse to recognize that this town is an integral part of my life, of my former self. The memories of my past live there. The memories of my family reside there.

And so, without awareness, I deny myself the obvious.

I refuse the intrinsic failure in my notion of escape.

But no matter, because, what I do allow inward, or rather *all* I allow inward, is my ever-strengthening pursuit of "happy." My need to go somewhere, *anywhere*, in search of it.

And soon enough, I make a friend!

Happily.

A friend…

Who, in all honesty, is nothing like me. Or rather, a friend who, in all ways suitable, is *every bit* me. This since she too wants to run from herself. She too has chosen a life postponed, stationary in the indefinite. She too runs from wearisome responsibilities and inconvenient adulthood.

Like me, she does this.

My new friend.

Who is every bit me…

Three months pass. She and I, we go out, listen to music. Enjoy dinner. Hike. For three months we share all this "happy."

Three satisfying months of happy, up until the time "happy" begins to fade.

She is a charmer, my new friend; she is a dazzler.

Up until the time she isn't.

Up until the time she emerges a liar and a thief, a con. My friend. *This* is who she is. And despite the voice within that has long struggled to warn me otherwise, I labor and I labor to guard our friendship. *Don't think, Sandra! Just enjoy!* Which I manage to convince myself I am pulling off. And which I make-believe I am successful in carrying out. For a bit. For far too long. Until it becomes impossible to no longer look the other way, I hold to her. For safety from myself.

Jewelry goes missing, clothes. A suitcase disappears. There is a day she wears a bracelet, a scarf. Both are mine. She wears these as we meet up. (I wouldn't notice?) She doesn't care. She locks my cat away for two fretful days. She progresses to destroy certain belongings.

She is my friend.

A sociopath.

A psychopath? Honestly, I don't know. What I do know, is that any sense of what is right and what is wrong is missing. A guiding voice within? This seems to differ from that of the most of us.

We are out to dinner. She tells me she misses her children. As for her husband, he has barred all contact, this with her three children…or was it four? It seems there are times I hear differently. But again, never mind, since it is stubbornly, inflexibly, *frantically*! that I hear consistency. This is what I hear because I have *profoundly, desperately, uncompromisingly*! blocked the voice that strains overtime, to alert me otherwise.

She is frightened, her children are frightened, of their father. Her ability to speak with a decipherable volume to her voice has now taken pause.

She wipes away silent tears.

And she needs money, my friend. This in order to win her children back. This in order to protect her three children (or possibly she will want to rescue all four), from their father.

He has seized all assets, this too is what this soulless man has done. He has frozen her out of every account.

Even those she had long possessed on her own…

I give her gifts then. She is grief-stricken, and I feel she needs this kindness. I believe this will do her well in escaping the unforeseen poverty she now suffers. If only for a moment. I offer sweaters, jewelry. A coat. I pay for meals. I do this blindly. I do this readily.

I do this obstinately!

"I *had* money." She is eager to reveal her *truthful* self. Her "beforehand" self, a time when her "otherness" was apparent, her status understood. She is incapable of recognizing the life in which she now finds herself.

She giggles next, her memories inspire this. Happily she recalls those earlier days, the extravagance she enjoyed then.

"There was a day…" Spontaneous laughter erupts from her. "A day when I spent thirty thousand dollars on a whim. I bought handbags and jewelry, makeup and scarves. All because I was in a mood, all because I could." Her face glows now.

This is what it does, until gradually her smile disappears. Before she sighs deeply. Again before the tears.

And do I believe her? Do I like her? Or rather…do I *will* myself to do both?

Yes, in desperation, I do just that.

And months go by as I do just that, as I will myself to believe, to trust, to *like*. Three months as I work tirelessly to suppress the ever-escalating shrill of the advisory voice within.

But it comes eventually, and yes, it comes too late, when I am no longer able to hold the voice at bay. Its pleading has become too strident, *ear splitting*! And as I break from her life this is the time she tells me that our friendship had meant nothing. My gifts…second rate. Suddenly she has come to realize she must surround herself with a higher quality people, she adds this "higher quality" with particular emphasis as she assesses me through a lens, newly focused, as now thankfully (*and just in time*!) she is enlightened as to the genuine me, the below-standard me. The embarrassment *of* me. Her look is proud as she considers all that is distasteful about me.

I smile to myself then, a bit weakly I do this. I wonder about my idiocy anew. The extent of the madness I have let in in pursuit of "happy." But too, the result of all this inane business, the fool-ishness I have passionately embraced, and every bit of the abuse I have greedily directed inward, is that soon enough I will replace all my circumvention of truth and reality, with the here and now and the present. And in lieu of flight, I will begin to reencounter the inevitable, with all its anguish, with all its painful hurdles. My friend, she gave me that opportunity. She provided that gift.

To face who I am.

That opportunity.

To admit what I must do.

That gift.

It meant nothing?

Whatever…

forty-nine

Going Home

And so I extract myself from all this friendship trauma, this mistreatment. And I do so with an understanding that I have now faced a new kind of defeat, a different sort of improper way to exist. I gather up my dog, my cat, my remaining and my unbroken belongings, and I return home in order to come to terms with my doctor and his intolerable instructions. And I go back to Robert despite my unalleviated anger. Home is where I go where, upon return, I will appreciatively encounter his newly imposed involvement with our daughter.

And I begin to write. I do this as a means to reappear into the here and now and the present, with all its painful memories and difficult sorting-through. And I hurt all over again as I relive the heartache of those years, the agony of the present. As I continue upward toward the air.

I will pause from this writing repeatedly. This occurs when I feel too much pain as it eddies around in order to draw me back under. I pause when these memories threaten, frighten. Because all this gradual thinking turned feeling, turned collapsing, this reaching inward toward the pain and catapulting away from distraction, all this is exhausting. Terrifying. Overwhelming. All this is hard.

But after years under water, I now have the opportunity to take in air if I want it.

And I want it.

fifty

What is Our Future?

Screw up, stumble. Nose dive. *Fail*!

"Please…will you try this?" I say this to Parker when I learn the reason for his disappearance. When I learn he has been working, *overworking*, all these years to save his father and rescue me from the sorrows delivered by the suffering of our oldest. So then I implore *this* of my son, all the disaster that could be his. Because our approval of him, our devotion to him, this will not waver. Despite anything that comes to be, *we* pledge to never let *him* down. Never will we do so again. So go ahead…*fail*. And at last know how it feels when, in doing so, you will not fail us.

But Parker, he doesn't stumble. His drive to succeed, his determination to do well through all his heartache, this does not lessen. Having changed disciplines to an area of study he desires rather than one he so long believed he must embrace in order to release his father, and to free me, from our grief, he regroups and once more he studies hard.

But before that time, before the time he will change disciplines, during the time he strives to find for himself what *he* wants for his future, he wanders a bit. He thinks, he considers much, until the time when, after three months away, he returns to the California Institute of Technology. And this is the time he asks the school if he can replace his former area of study and begin a new program. One that interests *him*. Excites *him*. One that pleases *him*.

And they say yes.

And this level of acceptance? This is noteworthy. But they want him in the face of all. He is brilliant. He is sought. And, like my oldest, he too is loved. Enormously loved.

And so he is granted his stay.

During the first week of homelessness, Grace shows at her father's office regularly. Since she is close by Robert, since Robert is close by her, she meanders the five quick blocks in order to reach the downtown core, in order to reach him. "Casually," then, she "drops by"; "Pops in!" to pay a visit. And Robert, he allows this indulging of her for that week. Until this "popping in" and this "dropping by" begins to seem ritual. This "Take me out to lunch" request starts to appear routine.

(*You're homeless Grace, remember?*)

But too, she is not family-less and, mercifully, she does remember that.

Nevertheless, Robert lays down the difficult mandate: "You cannot stop by here any longer."

And she stays away.

She must arrive at the shelter at 3:00 in the afternoon. Once there she will wait in a line outside the building among the displaced and the destitute, many of whom show outward signs of mental illness, and an intrusiveness that can so often accompany such a condition. An uncomfortable scene among uncomfortable people. But lingering out of doors, outside this facility, this is what is accessible for this line-up, no matter the weather. And this is what she must do every day, her sole option, if she wants to secure a bed for that night. Then too, she is required to leave the building, get back onto the pavement by 8:00 the next morning. An unbendable rule. No matter the flu, no matter any illness otherwise, setting aside the chilly air, she, alongside all the others, will go outside.

She is offered two meals a day, one in the morning and next in the evening. She is offered free counseling which can happen twice a week for up to two months' time. Her need to talk is enormous and she takes this up.

There comes a morning, as she waits in a line cafeteria-style, when she encounters a volunteer she knows serving breakfast. And this volunteer is someone with whom Grace attended high school. She is comforted by the presence of this girl, thankful to have in her surroundings a familiar face. A kind someone she can talk with.

And they do. They spend time in one another's company and they talk.

But in contrast, in *disgraceful opposition*, when I learn of this later, I am crushed. And (again) I feel incredible shame. Shame because I am humiliated by the exposure of the state in which my child has landed. And I feel disgrace, disgrace and dread, because our insensitive, cruel parenting has been exposed, as it stretches further outward. *Soon everyone from this school will know of our desertion and neglect, the void in place of where our hearts should exist.* Every student, each administrator, all faculty, and every parent...

All these people. From a school that is among a handful of high schools within the city where one is offered the best possible education...a school where no one "falls through the cracks." It just doesn't happen. Period. The education, the empowerment learned, the self-reliance acquired, all this is such that falling away? *This just doesn't happen.* But here is *my child* having fallen through. She is the one that falls. *The one.*

Therefore, instead of the too-small-amount of contentment I feel in learning she had a friend alongside her to furnish comfort during another difficult time, I feel humiliation. So shame on me.

For all my shortcomings. For all my setbacks.

For my humiliation.

Shame on me.

Throughout her homeless months Grace suspends hormonal treatment. The emotional instability brought about by replacement therapy is overpowering. Too difficult in her existing environment, too much while she attempts to survive parental abandonment.

And it comes that she suspends her treatments wisely, because abuse comes around to derail again. Verbal abuse, for certain. But too, this is the time physical abuse eventually arrives. As she has stopped the hormone treatments, the treatments, I will later learn, she had taken sporadically at best, she continues to not appear as the female person she is. And this "not-appearing-female" dilemma is the reason that others are angry when she is allowed a bed in the female side of the shelter. As such, there comes an evening when a group of women, some of whom are escaping violent men, surround her. And they scream at her, push her, shove her, kick her, and hit her. Then they scream at her some more.

And I am away during all this. I am "*happy*" during all this; therefore I am unaware any of this has occurred. And so I cannot protect her. I have no idea she needs protection from this. And moreover, had I been around, there would be no allowing my shielding her from this. No intervention. "*She must raise herself up.*" This is how tough our tough love must be. And this stay-ing-out-of-it would have been impossible if not for the fact that I am away, if not for the fact that I am uninformed. Hard-heart-edly, all during this period, I am adrift just as she is adrift. And, in being so, I forsake my child.

But the shelter staff, they do race to rescue her. The pack of violent women is thrown back onto the streets, immediately. And the shelter, this will be unavailable to them for the next three weeks. Forever, if it happens again.

Nevertheless Grace is shaken. Phobias threaten to upend again. And, as a result, the morning following, she shows at her father's office once more. And she sobs, and she trembles, and *he* must step up. Her fear, her panic, this cannot be evaded. I am now unavailable and, as such, no longer can *he check out*. And he sees that he must put aside work. Which he does. And he embraces her while she cries. Then they talk. Then she rests at his office all that day before he takes her home. Despite our doctor's instructions, he takes her home. And when I learn of this later, I am grateful.

But this being at home? This night spent in her own bed

surrounded by her father's protection? This will be only the one night. Because again, *she* must raise *herself* up. *She will learn to be self-sufficient.* Therefore this is the impossible action he must take, and does take, the following morning…he puts her back on the streets.

Her brother, her grandparents, her aunts and her uncles, her cousins, friends, all have been instructed to condemn her to the streets as well. No coddling, under any circumstances. *She* will raise *herself, by herself, she* will end this continuous failing; *she* will get *herself* to a state of autonomy. This, *she herself* will do…even if in the meantime it threatens to destroy the rest of us. Which it does.

Having been banned from the refuge of her father's office Grace seeks somewhere, anywhere she can place herself other than the streets. She chooses then the downtown branch of our city's library. This is now the spot where she will spend her homeless daytime hours until it's time for the 3:00 line-up. This is where she will warm herself from the October chill, with its persistent dampness, and progressively cooler temperatures.

And *this* is where, and *this* is when, she gets to work. She advantages herself of the rows of available computers there. She writes to her various doctors, both those on campus, as well as those away. She does this there. And these doctors of psychology/psychiatry, they furnish written details providing explanations as to the intervals she wasn't able to make school work. Reasons as to poor grades. Clarifications as to times dropped out.

Former professors are sought too. Those she had known intimately. These individuals too agree to write on her behalf. They highlight her brilliance, they affirm what her various doctors have said, reasons as to her failings. They understand she has a desire to study, this despite all the earlier withdrawals. These instructors are mindful of the struggles against which she has battled. They are aware of her challenges, her upward climbs, her downward plummets. And they don't judge. Markedly contrasting the medical physicians in that small town, those she had earlier approached for female hormones, they do not pass judgement. They encourage forward movement, upward rising. And, as such, this is the manner in which she puts her supportive team in place. Then she speaks with the registrar. And this is how *she* gets *herself* back in school.

On her own.

♣

"*She has the instinct for survival,*" remember? The nurses, a lifetime ago, they had told me this as "he" lay slowly maturing inside his box of glass.

So with holding that memory in our hearts we continue our tough love. This again at our doctor's insistence. Never again the coddling. We will no longer anguish over the prospect of suicide. We hold to this, to that which was said well over two decades ago, or, more precisely, twenty-seven years back, nearly to the day, about our newborn "son." And we hold to this because we have now seen that she has taken steps on her own. And we do this, because we must.

We will not pay expenses. This is now what our psychologist presses us on. Setting this further mandate, this is the time…this is over the time.

She will find, on her own, a manner in which to pay both her tuition, as well as her living expenses. Period.

And so again we do the difficult.

For her.

fifty-one

Parker

In our quest to spend more time with Parker, now that we fully realize the problem we have created, we decide to take a trip. Just the three of us, Robert, Parker, and me. Since a technical climb up a mountain is beyond, way beyond any ability I have, seeing as though Robert has not climbed a mountain in thirty long years, but then, given that Parker has made mountains, and the climbing of them, his passion…we want a mountain.

Parker then suggests the perfect one: a mountain where no technical skills will be required of its climbers. There will be no roping up in order to traverse a glacier, no need to burden ourselves with cumbersome crampons; not one unexpected crevasse will appear before us. There will exist no threat of avalanche. In fact, no snow or ice will stretch across our path, ever.

Truthfully then, it's not a climb at all. Instead we will hike. But this hike, this will not be short-lived. This hike? This will be sixty full miles. Simply told, it is not miniscule, this mountain. In contrast, its height extends 19,341 feet coming to crest in the thin, dizzying air. And too, it is the highest peak in Africa. One of seven mountains, on seven continents, that Parker will then cross off his list. Flawless.

So with Parker in mind we wind our way up Kilimanjaro. It takes nine days. Nine days, without a shower. Nine days, as quickly we run out of warm, soothing, caffeinated chocolate. Nine days, during which we span three climate zones. We pass through a rainforest, muddy, inches deep. A sticky, slippery, sucking our boots under forest of mud. We traverse plains, and on these plains open wide? There exists no bush, no presence of a simple boulder, to offer privacy from the *sixteen male* porters, the *two male* guides, and my *two male* family members, all with me on the trail. (Everyone about-face! For me! *Yes, it's true, one more about-face. For me. Yet again…*)

We scramble up and over boulders moving at a crawl. (Save for Parker.) At times we tread for miles straight uphill when switchbacks do not present themselves. Parker is asked to move slowly, at a pace the guides have set in order to protect against the dizzy sickness high altitudes can bring on, the risk of it greater when ascending too fast. But Parker is impatient with this. He is not used to moving leisurely while on mountains or elsewhere. So as he decelerates he brings to mind someone who rides a bike while pedaling too slowly and is in danger of losing balance, of tumbling over. "Are you about to fall sideways?" I ask him. He smiles. He suggests we play word games when the days' walks become long. We entertain ourselves by this. The guides too are amused.

Then, on the seventh day, the day we summit? The day all drinking water freezes…one long day spilling over into night as we start our final ascent minutes before midnight, this in advance of our two days' descent, after which I will lose both large toenails, it is cold. *Very cold*. Fifteen below *cold*. In spite of my five impenetrable coverings, which when added comprise polypropylene layers (seemingly fit to *me*, as if made to meld with *my* skin exclusively), this followed by woolly fleece (densely woven, hugging-me-closely wooly fleece), I have a layer of down (*substantially* big, puffy down), and I wear Gortex (prepared for wind, chill or wet, ready to stand against whichever, or all at once, possible high mountain elements, Gortex). But, despite all this fortification. I am *cold*!

Then too, yet given the beauty as we summit, which reveals the arc of the world at sunrise, a pink, turned magenta, giving over to purple band of color, a virtual semicircle "embracing-the-Earth rainbow" peeking slowly, rising shyly over the outline of our planet. Despite the dreamlike layer of clouds miles upon miles below which, when looked upon, appear as a distant lavender ocean…in spite of the sloping glaciers to our side, which are also a sight surreal as gently they progress through shades of purple. And finally, despite my appreciation for all this magnificence, this otherworldly awe, and although I have fantastically accomplished this feat, I want down, because *it is cold*. Because *I am cold*. And I am dizzy, a stumbling about, "walking dead" sluggish shuffle, oxygen deprived, bad for the brain, no way to access full logic, altitude dizzy. And so, I not only want down, I need down. Now!

Gradually then on our descent, our iced water returns to its original liquid form. But although we have been awake, hiking, scrambling, and not eating since midnight, we continue our downward trek until 2:00 the following afternoon. Fourteen hours of fasting and continuous plodding downward.

Then we pause. For a meal. A warm drink. A momentary respite. Before our guides inform we will get moving again. We don't stop then until 6:00 that evening. My feet ache. My toe-nails hurt.

But I am happy.

The last morning we are wakened early, very early. So that after trekking ten miles more to arrive at the base, assembling into the waiting van, and having been dropped off at our hotel, it is now barely 10:00 in the morning.

I sit on the veranda, boots off, feet up...my blackened toe-nails hanging sideways while I ask Parker if he would search for a glass of gin mixed with anything. He grins and goes inside. Although before entering the bar he turns back. He then coins a term, a variation on the expected that will, from this moment forward, become our family standard no matter the circumstances.

"Sure Mom, it's 10:00 AM somewhere."

It is. I lean back, and I smile too.

fifty-two

Grace

Before school will start in January Grace is allowed back home throughout the two months' wait. It is then, during this time home, that she meets someone. A someone whom she is long due to have in her life.

She and Katherine had found one another on a match-making site. The two had written for a week, and next they met up for coffee. They talked, they played chess. They went to dinner. They saw each other twice more that week.

And they become inseparable. Lovers. This then is the moment we learn our daughter is bisexual. And this is also the time we learn that, with transgender individuals, this being "bi," this is exceedingly common. So her love, she too is a woman.

And this girlfriend? Remarkably, she is set to attend the same university as our daughter in January.

As for Grace? This is the time she turns into someone we haven't known for two decades. She evolves into, emerges as, someone happy! Exceptionally joyful! So of course Robert and I are delighted too. And, as we breathe in this new peace, this reprieve, we allow ourselves to relax. Because it is wonderful to see her experience this. Perfect to see, to *feel*, freedom from the endless other.

But again…here is another catch…incessantly the bumpy path forward. And at needless and painful cost to both Grace and Katherine, because Katherine's parents see gay, lesbian, bisexual as something fake. They see transgender as a lie. An "if you would simply try harder, you would then be just like the rest of us," falsity. "*The dire need for conformity is not generation-specific.*"

As for my child, there will be hurt, again too much hurt, as she observes the pain her girlfriend must endure, as she herself suffers more rejection. And this rejection? This is for the simple reason that she lives an honest existence. This is for the reason that she is genuine to herself and because she presents herself as genuine to others. Her life, this complicated life…a life where she "*does the right thing even when no one's looking.*" The life she will end if she cannot live it sincerely.

This continuous battle is punishing, this is excessive. This is her unremitting fight for survival. And now she has been faced with two additional others, two others who are tremendously important to her girlfriend, against whom she must, all over again, endure.

Desperately my wish is to dispel the beliefs of these people, these parents that reject the veracity inherent in being gay, lesbian, bisexual, gender fluid, and transgender, the honesty of it. My daughter's immense suffering, her inability to truly live. Her thoughts of suicide. Her years of neediness and desperation. This, all of this…this is not fake.

But in the face of all that is true, if the two are to continue as one, live as a couple happily, then Katherine will no longer be given money to continue her education. She will no longer be given means to pay rent.

But she endures this.

They both endure this.

And, at least for the present, it will be our family alone that will embrace their relationship. We will validate their love. Support them. And, in return, they will devote time to us. They will celebrate each holiday with us.

Our gain then.

And, all over again...*at least there's that.*

Once back in academia Grace engages, fiercely so, in her studies. Her classes, they matter a lot. And she is happy as concerns her personal life. But as involves the wider picture? In order to make school happen at present, she continues to forego hormone therapy. By now she is aware that inseparable from hormone treatment are the ups and downs, the continuous backs and forths. Taking them will rapidly springboard toward emotional havoc. She knows this. She has lived this. Already. And the intrusiveness of these emotions, the instability they will produce will render ineffective any cognitive ability she may otherwise have. An obstacle impossible to maneuver around.

And so together with all this inevitable mind obstruction, this unavoidable falling apart, the managing of school and any requirements associated with it will prove too difficult. Too impossibly difficult. Always there emerges a something which is too very difficult.

Because transgender, *this* is difficult; *this*, in fact, is way bigger than something difficult. This is *immensely* bigger than that.

Therefore she will undergo one feat at a time. That is it. That is all she can bring about. And for now, she has chosen school. "Change," this will come later.

And again the learning. My limitless enlightenment which climbs anew only to teach me that this tackling of only one goings-on at a time is as good as built-in among transgender people. Because transgender is difficult; because *transformation* is difficult. *Transformation* is way beyond something difficult.

Transformation is miles added to miles added to miles beyond that.

It is around this same time that we purchase a car. Robert will drive this car. And, as follows, the handing-over of his former vehicle is reoffered, the notion of a driver's license reexamined. She is twenty-seven. Parker, he had received his car at twenty-two, this as soon as his undergraduate work in Minnesota had come to completion. This is the car he had used to get himself to Maine the summer he had worked on the lobster boat. This he had used when driving to Wyoming the following winter in order to ski (outside the boundaries and safety of the resort). And this is the car he next drove to Pasadena so as to follow up on his studies.

But as for Grace? There are certain fears, more precisely there are certain *phobias*, to which she still cowers. Driving is one of these. But…as for Katherine? She *wants* to drive this car. Very much she wants this car around. Therefore Robert makes the deal. Knowing he has leverage, he sets down this ruling:

Grace has one month to get her license, four weeks unnegotiable, in which to do so. This, in order to have the car, the car Kathrine is eager, think bursting, to use.

That's it. End of discussion. One month! Or no car.

So then impossible child of mine, you *will* conquer your fear of this driving of cars, or you will wildly disappoint your girlfriend.

Given this quandary, *which will you choose?*

The two up north launch into practice.

Practicing driving? This is something I had previously helped with many times in earlier years. At times when allowed. Intervals she wasn't lying prone. This repetition, this I felt *I should do* over the many earlier years, this as a means to help her overcome at least one of her uncontrollable leg shaking, bringing-forth-a-panic-attack fears. But now? Now I have no further patience with this…this helping her out. This laying down of a law only to watch her disregard it. *This* is for which I have no more patience. Moreover, seeing as though I am the singular person who cannot make one difference as concerns change…ever and forever I have *not an ounce of influence*, I have no desire to think about patience. And too, as remembered, and as already lived, from the time I was instructed to lay down the driving law… *No one to date has any idea what I'm up against*, and so yes, without dilemma, I will bow out.

But Grace and Kathrine continue on. They rehearse. They repeat. They practice and they prepare. Over and over they do this. Until the day of the test.

Which Grace then passes.

And which is the reason Robert inhales. And as for indifferent me? Well, I then take a tedious breath too.

She will be nearly thirty when she receives her bachelor's degree in computer science. Along with a minor in mathematics.

And this computer science degree, this will be from a state, from one of a few particular schools within this state, where computer science programs are given resources enough so as to be nationally competitive.

And despite her thirty years, regardless of the many years within that thirty-year spectrum when she had faced habitual suffering and routine disappointment, she will now have lifted her grade point average to just a trace below a full 4.0. This is what she is able to accomplish during this current period of study. Moreover, this grade point average, this is factored into her former average which, just as in high school, consistently sagged somewhere within the lower 2s. This "before average," this is the average she received from the handful of grades, from the handful of classes in which she managed to remain until the end, when all she was capable was to stay just above the probation line. Or "stay" not at all. That was the best average then.

But now? Now is the period she has devised computer programs, unlocked computer codes and created computer languages, all done where, at times, she is openly acknowledged for surpassing a level of proficiency and sophistication greater than those of her professors.

And there is more.

This newfound success? Yes, this continues...

As she has been recruited...

Two months before receiving her degree, she is recruited to work for the same company that, when in high school, she had suggested twelve improvements to their game. The twelve they immediately implemented. Over this past year she had devised yet more changes, more upgrading, which again were welcomed and put into operation. And so, as follows, this position they are offering up? This is not modest…this is not entry level.

She tells this company, a company rated within the top ten tech companies worldwide, that she plans to finish school. She has two more months.

They hold the position.

And so this is good work, this is long-awaited good work. And this would be true at any age. Even if stepping up to and crossing over the finish line will have taken eleven, or more accurately…thirty…full years.

Finally, this is good work.

afterword

Forgiveness. This is something big. Forgiveness. It will lighten you, lift you up. Literally. Forgiveness, this will give you a "spring" long forgotten, a "bounce" neglected. A life less burdened. Even joy, it will give this too. I have come to know this firsthand.

And the trick? Do it for yourself, forgiveness. Do it with those who have caused you harm, and others who have caused you pain. Do it for your own well-being. For the return of "happy." Do it in order to recover a spring years lost. Then hold to it. Faithfully.

I have forgiven friends and teachers, family members who, over these baffling years, have offered advice. Advice that often cut to the core. Those competent others who had sound guidelines as to proper parenting, unsolicited counsel on ways to correct my wrongs. This hurt, at times immensely.

And too, this guidance? This mixed confusingly with the profound guilt of the muddle I was told, and sorely felt, I alone had created. How did these others know how to do it? Why didn't I have the mothering instinct? *Why couldn't I give the look that would freeze my child in "his" tracks?* These others, they were overfilled

with information as to the clear way out of the mess I had created, if only I would do things right. But I believe, and I believe
sincerely, they meant no harm. And I forgive them.

And I do so for me.

I forgive the doctor who would have, could have, should have,
told me years back my child felt to be female. I forgive him for
the years of confusion we barely endured. I forgive him for the
hurt created by his silence, the endless despair.

This forgiveness, this is harder, but I do it, and I do it for the
return of joy.

I forgive the psychiatrist who told me, in no ambiguous terms,
that as soon as I get better, my "son" will get better. The endless
guilt his words had spawned within, the hopelessness. I forgive
him for having me believe that my child's suffering had been sin-
glehandedly my fault. My failure. Alone. Then my poor attempts
to "buck up," which were years ineffective. And I embraced this
judgement. It was me who continued to be the cause of "Grant's"
misery. This I was reminded of over and over.

But I forgive him, because for too long I have been unhappy,
and I want happy back.

I forgive the writing instructor, a woman I have known since
the age of five. A woman I had trusted. I forgive her for her
callous judgement and for her inflated sense of unquestionable

insight into the hearts and the minds of others. I forgive her for her quick assumptions and her disregard to learn the whole picture. For the added and senseless pain this caused me.

I do this to recover from my years of sorrow and confusion.

I do this for bounce.

I do this for joy.

I forgive the two others who caused me pain through ignorance: the man in the truck who unreservedly furthered my heartache. I forgive the clerk in the grocery who willingly directed every bit of his misguided rage toward me.

I forgive them too.

I forgive the parents of my daughter's girlfriend and all others who stand by the injurious belief that LBGTQ people live an imprudent life. A life they could adjust if only they had the courage to try harder, if only they possessed stronger moral fiber. They would do this. If only.

I forgive them for not seeing that my child is the bravest person they will ever encounter. That her suffering is real and that who she loves is genuine. I forgive them for the stringent moral code they adhere to. The hurt this moral code causes my daughter. The hurt this moral code causes within me, for the hatred this code fosters throughout the world. I forgive them to lighten the weight of the pain I shoulder.

I forgive them for me.

I forgive Robert who, for many years, too often avoided what should have been a shared emotional role in caring for Grace. His circumvention. His too-often looking the other way. I forgive him for all the despair I barely endured as our child's problems were destroying her, destroying me, crushing the two of us bit by bit. I forgive him because, through his embraces and reassurance, he felt he was doing for me what I needed. Because he truly was unable to hear me. Because his work justly put him out of town. Because he never meant to further my hurt. Because in the end, he did the difficult task of offering assistance or rather, the *very difficult task* of *not* offering assistance, as a means to give our daughter the gift of self-reliance.

I forgive him for us. I forgive him for me. I forgive him because I love him, and I forgive him for spring.

I forgive myself. I pardon me for the too many battles fought between my daughter and me. The battles that I was responsible to quell but was unable. I forgive myself for not "bucking up." For my helplessness and my hopelessness. My staring off into space. For too often failing to model the behavior I wanted. For the pills, the impatience, the accusations. I forgive myself in order to nurture my child's well-being. I do this for both of us and for our future. I do this for bounce. And I do this for joy.

In all the struggles we have faced, the battles and the tears, our burdens, all of which have led to a nearly broken marriage, years of pain and uncertainty, it is Parker who was continuously left behind. While being the "together child," the easy child, he was pushed to an unreachable part of my mind. (*And how is it I was never able to see that he was, in fact, not fine, as I had always perceived*? *Had always believed*? Had always *needed* to believe…)

How?

And so forgiving myself for neglecting his needs? This is something other. This is daunting. This plagues me every moment. This is something I, as of yet, have been unable to do. It is his turn now, and for a long time forward it will continue to be his spotlight. He is now the one who is inside my head continuously. I do not know if I will ever make it better for him. I do not know if he will ever feel my endless, infinite love.

But I will try. Unendingly I will do this. This is my primary worry, my distress. My goal. And no, I have not forgiven myself for the pain I have caused him. This forgiveness? This may prove insurmountable. His pain, my own pain regarding his. This is something I may never accomplish. But I will try for him. And I will try for us. With that in mind I will try.

A Bit of Reverie
A Touch of Nostalgia
A Little Ache

I remember him, my son. His early birth, our fear. His laughter, his smiles. His anguish, and his fight. My memories, of course, include his brilliance, a brilliance that remains today. The type of which places her yet further from the norm.

I remember him.

But the memories we build today, these are of a different sort. And, as before, they include my child. We amass them today, we will tomorrow. We will build them the next, and at all times moving forward.

But these memories, they won't include him. And I miss him.

These memories will be strictly of her. And I'm lucky to have her.

I embrace them both, Grant *and* Grace.

I am fortunate to be with Grace, to see her. To touch her. To love her. She is my present and my future.

And although Grant will remain out of sight, all I need to do is look back and I can see him and I can love him too.

Sandra Bowman, her husband Robert and their
labrador retriever Charlee divide their time between
Seattle, Washington and Ketchum, Idaho.